WORLD BANK TECHNICAL PAPER NO. 482

Europe and Central Asia Poverty Reduction and Economic Management Series

Trade and Cost Competitiveness in the Czech Republic, Hungary, Poland, and Slovenia

Peter Havlik

Recent World Bank Technical Papers

No. 408 Donovan and Frank, *Soil Fertility Management in Sub-Saharan Africa*

No. 409 Heggie and Vickers, *Commercial Management and Financing of Roads*

No. 410 Sayeg, *Successful Conversion to Unleaded Gasoline in Thailand*

No. 411 Calvo, *Options for Managing and Financing Rural Transport Infrastructure*

No. 413 Langford, Forster, and Malcolm, *Toward a Financially Sustainable Irrigation System: Lessons from the State of Victoria, Australia, 1984–1994*

No. 414 Salman and Boisson de Chazournes, *International Watercourses: Enhancing Cooperation and Managing Conflict, Proceedings of a World Bank Seminar*

No. 415 Feitelson and Haddad, *Identification of Joint Management Structures for Shared Aquifers: A Cooperative Palestinian-Israeli Effort*

No. 416 Miller and Reidinger, eds., *Comprehensive River Basin Development: The Tennessee Valley Authority*

No. 417 Rutkowski, *Welfare and the Labor Market in Poland: Social Policy during Economic Transition*

No. 418 Okidegbe and Associates, *Agriculture Sector Programs: Sourcebook*

No. 420 Francis and others, *Hard Lessons: Primary Schools, Community, and Social Capital in Nigeria*

No. 421 Gert Jan Bom, Robert Foster, Ebel Dijkstra, and Marja Tummers, *Evaporative Air-Conditioning: Applications for Environmentally Friendly Cooling*

No. 422 Peter Quaak, Harrie Knoef, and Huber Stassen, *Energy from Biomass: A Review of Combustion and Gasification Technologies*

No. 423 Energy Sector Unit, Europe and Central Asia Region, World Bank, *Non-Payment in the Electricity Sector in Eastern Europe and the Former Soviet Union*

No. 424 Jaffee, ed., *Southern African Agribusiness: Gaining through Regional Collaboration*

No. 425 Mohan, ed., *Bibliography of Publications: Africa Region, 1993–98*

No. 426 Rushbrook and Pugh, *Solid Waste Landfills in Middle- and Lower-Income Countries: A Technical Guide to Planning, Design, and Operation*

No. 427 Mariño and Kemper, *Institutional Frameworks in Successful Water Markets: Brazil, Spain, and Colorado, USA*

No. 428 C. Mark Blackden and Chitra Bhanu, *Gender, Growth, and Poverty Reduction: Special Program of Assistance for Africa, 1998 Status Report on Poverty in Sub-Saharan Africa*

No. 429 Gary McMahon, José Luis Evia, Alberto Pascó-Font, and José Miguel Sánchez, *An Environmental Study of Artisanal, Small, and Medium Mining in Bolivia, Chile, and Peru*

No. 430 Maria Dakolias, *Court Performance around the World: A Comparative Perspective*

No. 431 Severin Kodderitzsch, *Reforms in Albanian Agriculture: Assessing a Sector in Transition*

No. 432 Luiz Gabriel Azevedo, Musa Asad, and Larry D. Simpson, *Management of Water Resources: Bulk Water Pricing in Brazil*

No. 433 Malcolm Rowat and José Astigarraga, *Latin American Insolvency Systems: A Comparative Assessment*

No. 434 Csaba Csaki and John Nash, eds., *Regional and International Trade Policy: Lessons for the EU Accession in the Rural Sector—World Bank/FAO Workshop, June 20–23, 1998*

No. 435 Iain Begg, *EU Investment Grants Review*

No. 436 Roy Prosterman and Tim Hanstad, ed., *Legal Impediments to Effective Rural Land Relations in Eastern Europe and Central Asia: A Comparative Perspective*

No. 437 Csaba Csaki, Michel Dabatisse, and Oskar Honisch, *Food and Agriculture in the Czech Republic: From a "Velvet" Transition to the Challenges of EU Accession*

No. 438 George J. Borjas, *Economic Research on the Determinants of Immigration: Lessons for the European Union*

No. 439 Mustapha Nabli, *Financial Integration, Vulnerabilities to Crisis, and EU Accession in Five Central European Countries*

No. 440 Robert Bruce, Ioannis Kessides, and Lothar Kneifel, *Overcoming Obstacles to Liberalization of the Telecom Sector in Estonia, Poland, the Czech Republic, Slovenia, and Hungary: An Overview of Key Policy Concerns and Potential Initiatives to Facilitate the Transition Process*

No. 441 Bartlomiej Kaminski, *Hungary: Foreign Trade Issues in the Context of Accession to the EU*

No. 442 Bartlomiej Kaminski, *The Role of Foreign Direct Investment and Trade Policy in Poland's Accession to the European Union*

(List continues on the inside back cover)

WORLD BANK TECHNICAL PAPER NO. 482
Europe and Central Asia Poverty Reduction and Economic Management Series

Trade and Cost Competitiveness in the Czech Republic, Hungary, Poland, and Slovenia

Peter Havlik

The World Bank
Washington, D.C.

Copyright © 2000
The International Bank for Reconstruction
and Development/THE WORLD BANK
1818 H Street, N.W.
Washington, D.C. 20433, U.S.A.

Technical Papers are published to communicate the results of the Bank's work to the development community with the least possible delay. The typescript of this paper therefore has not been prepared in accordance with the procedures appropriate to formal printed texts, and the World Bank accepts no responsibility for errors. Some sources cited in this paper may be informal documents that are not readily available.

The findings, interpretations, and conclusions expressed in this paper are entirely those of the author(s) and should not be attributed in any manner to the World Bank, to its affiliated organizations, or to members of its Board of Executive Directors or the countries they represent. The World Bank does not guarantee the accuracy of the data included in this publication and accepts no responsibility for any consequence of their use. The boundaries, colors, denominations, and other information shown on any map in this volume do not imply on the part of the World Bank Group any judgment on the legal status of any territory or the endorsement or acceptance of such boundaries.

The material in this publication is copyrighted. The World Bank encourages dissemination of its work and will normally grant permission promptly.

Permission to photocopy items for internal or personal use, for the internal or personal use of specific clients, or for educational classroom use, is granted by the World Bank, provided that the appropriate fee is paid directly to Copyright Clearance Center, Inc., 222 Rosewood Drive, Danvers, MA 01923, U.S.A., telephone 978-750-8400, fax 978-750-4470. Please contact the Copyright Clearance Center before photocopying items.

For permission to reprint individual articles or chapters, please fax your request with complete information to the Republication Department, Copyright Clearance Center, fax 978-750-4470.

All other queries on rights and licenses should be addressed to the World Bank at the address above or faxed to 202-522-2422.

ISBN: 0-8213-4796-9
ISSN: 0253-7494

Peter Havlik is deputy director, and senior researcher at the Vienna Institute for International Economic Studies (WIIW).

Library of Congress Cataloging-in-Publication Data

Havlik, Peter.
    Trade and cost competitiveness in the Czech Republic, Hungary, Poland, and Slovenia
      p.   cm. — (World Bank technical paper ; no. 482)
    Includes bibliographical references
    ISBN 0-8213-4796-9
    1. Europe, Eastern—Economic conditions—1989.
    2. Europe, Eastern—Economic conditions—1989—Statistics.
    3. Europe, Central—Economic conditions.   4. Europe, Central—Economic conditions—Statistics.
    5. Competition—Europe, Eastern. 6. Competition—Europe, Central   .I. Title   II. Series.

HC244.H375   2000
382'.0943—dc21

00-043636
CIP

Contents

Foreword vii
Abstract viii
Executive Summary ix
1. Labor Costs and Productivity 1
    Wages: Domestic and International Developments 1
    Productivity and Unit Labor Costs 10
    Productivity and Unit Labor Costs Levels in Manufacturing Industry 15
2. Trade Specialization and Competitiveness of Manufacturing Industry 20
    Central and Eastern European Countries' Competitive Export Industries .. 20
    Emerging Specialization Patterns of Central and Eastern European Countries'
    Exports 23
    The Changing Pattern of the Central and Eastern European Countries' Revealed
    Comparative Advantage 27
3. Foreign Direct Investment, Restructuring, and Competitiveness 30
    Foreign and Domestic Sectors Compared 30
    Conclusions and Policy Recommendations 33
Notes 36
Annex A 39
Annex B 43
Annex C 51
Annex D 55
Annex E 59
References 61

Tables

Table 1   Gross Wages and Salaries Per Month Per Employee, Total, European Currency
          Units at Exchange Rate 2
Table 2   Wages, Productivity, and Unit Labor Costs (ULCs), 1990–98 (Annual changes in
          percent) 6
Table 3   Monthly Gross Wages in the Manufacturing Industry, 1997 (Manufacturing = 100) . 10
Table 4   Central and Eastern European Aggregate Wages, Productivity and ULCs in 1996
          (Austria = 100) 13
Table 5   Unit Labor Costs (UlCs) in Industry (Wages/Productivity), Exchange Rate (ECU)
          Adjusted (Change in percent against preceding year) 15
Table 6   Productivity in the Manufacturing Industry, 1996 (Manufacturing = 100) 16
Table 7a   International Comparison of Total Labor Costs in the Manufacturing Industry
          (1996, PPP for GDP, Austria = 100) 18

Table 7b   International Comparison of Total Labor Costs in the Manufacturing Industry (1996, PPP for Gross Fixed Capital Formation, Austria = 100) 18

Table 8   European Union (12)—Manufacturing Industry Imports from Central and Eastern European Countries, European Currency Unit millions (Without intra-EU trade) 22

Table 9   Central and Eastern European Countries' Market Share in European Union (12) Manufacturing Industry Imports (Without intra-EU trade) 22

Table 10   European Union (12)—Manufacturing Industry Exports to Central and Eastern European Countries, European Currency Unit Millions (Without intra-EU trade) 22

Table 11   Central and Eastern European Countries' Shares in European Union (12) Manufacturing Industry Exports (Without intra-EU trade) 23

Table 12   Central and Eastern European Countries' Trade Balances in Manufacturing Industry Trade with the European Union (12), European Currency Unit Millions 23

Table 13   X-Factor Intensities of Central and Eastern European Countries' Most Competitive Industries in Exports to the European Union (12), 1993–97 (Average x-factor intensity of top 50 competitive industries in percent of average for all 92 industries) 25

Table 14   Foreign Investment Enterprises (FIEs) in Percent of All Manufacturing Industry Companies, 1997 31

Figures

Figure 1   Wage and Productivity Development Czech Republic (1989 = 100) 3
Figure 2   Wage and Productivity Development Hungary (1989 = 100) 3
Figure 3   Wage and Productivity Development Poland (1989 = 100) 4
Figure 4   Wage and Productivity Development Slovenia (1989 = 100) 4
Figure 5   Exchange Rate Deviation Indexes (ERDI = ER/PPP, National Currency Per ECU) ..5
Figure 6   Unit Labor Costs (ULCs), Exchange Rate (ECU) Adjusted (1989 = 100) 7
Figure 7   Wage Dispersion (Manufacturing = 100) 9
Figure 8   Unit Labor Costs (European Currency Unit–Adjusted), Annual Growth Rates in Percent 12
Figure 9   International Comparison of Unit Labor Costs (ULCs), PPP Adjusted (Austria = 100) 14
Figure 10   Correlation of X-Factor Intensities and Export Growth to the EU (12) for 50 Most Competitive Industries, 1993–97 26
Figure 11   Correlation of X-Factor Intensities and Market Shares in EU (12) for 50 Most Competitive Industries in 1997 26
Figure 12   Correlation of X-Factor Intensities with Revealed Comparative Advantage Values in Trade with the European Union (12), 1989–97 28

Figure 13 Czech Republic: Unit Labor Cost Growth (ECU) and Foreign Penetration 35
Figure 14 Hungary: Unit Labor Cost Growth (ECU) and Foreign Penetration 35

Annexes

Table A.1   Prices, Exchange Rates, and Unit Labor Costs (ULC), 1990–98 (ECU-based
               annual averages) 39
Table A.2   Wages, Productivity, and Unit Labor Costs (ULCs), 1990–98 (Annual
               changes in percent) 41
Table B.1.1   Czech Republic—Production Growth (Annual changes in percent) 43
Table B.1.2   Czech Republic—Employment Growth (Annual changes in percent) 43
Table B.1.3   Czech Republic—Average Monthly Gross Wages (ECU) (Annual changes in
               percent) 43
Table B.1.4   Czech Republic—Labor Productivity (Annual changes in percent) 44
Table B.1.5   Czech Republic—Unit Labor Costs (ECU) (Annual changes in percent) ...44
Table B.1.6   Czech Republic—Direct and Indirect Labor Costs (1996 in percent) 44
Table B.2.1   Hungary—Production Growth (Annual changes in percent) 45
Table B.2.2   Hungary—Employment Growth (Annual changes in percent) 45
Table B.2.3   Hungary—Average Monthly Gross Wages (ECU) (Annual changes in
               percent) 45
Table B.2.4   Hungary—Labor Productivity (Annual changes in percent) 46
Table B.2.5   Hungary—Unit Labor Costs (ECU) (Annual changes in percent) 46
Table B.2.6   Hungary—Direct and Indirect Labor Costs, 1995–97 (In percent) 46
Table B.3.1   Poland—Production Growth (Annual changes in percent) 47
Table B.3.2   Poland—Employment Growth (Annual changes in percent) 47
Table B.3.3   Poland—Average Monthly Gross Wages (ECU) (Annual changes
               in percent) 47
Table B.3.4   Poland—Labor Productivity (Annual changes in percent) 48
Table B.3.5   Poland—Unit Labor Costs (ECU) (Annual changes in percent) 48
Table B.3.6   Poland—Direct and Indirect Labor Costs (1996 in percent) 48
Table B.4.1   Slovenia—Production Growth (Annual changes in percent) 49
Table B.4.2   Slovenia—Employment Growth (Annual changes in percent) 49
Table B.4.3   Slovenia—Average Monthly Gross Wages (ECU) (Annual changes
               in percent) 49
Table B.4.4   Slovenia—Labor Productivity (Annual changes in percent) 50
Table B.4.5   Slovenia—Unit Labor Costs (ECU) (Annual changes in percent) 50
Table C.1   Czech Republic—Gaining and Losing Industries in Exports to the European
               Union(12), 1993–97 51
Table C.2   Hungary—Gaining and Losing Industries in Exports to the European Union
               (12), 1993–97 52

Table C.3   Poland—Gaining and Losing Industries in Exports to the European Union
             (12), 1993–97 53
Table C.4   Slovenia—Gaining and Losing Industries in Exports to the European Union
             (12), 1993–97 54
Table D.1   Czech Republic—Revealed Comparative Advantage Values 55
Table D.2   Hungary—Revealed Comparative Advantage Values 56
Table D.3   Poland—Revealed Comparative Advantage Values 57
Table D.4   Slovenia—Revealed Comparative Advantage Values 58
Table E.1   Nominal Capital (FIEs share in the total of the manufacturing industries,
             1996, percent and percentage point change, 1994–96) 59
Table E.2   Employed Persons (FIEs share in the total of the manufacturing industries,
             1996, percent and percentage point change, 1994–96) 59
Table E.3   Sales (FIEs share in the total of the manufacturing industries, 1996, percent
             and percentage point change, 1994–96) 60
Table E.4   Export Sales (FIEs share in the total of the manufacturing industries, 1996,
             percent and percentage point change, 1994–96) 60

Foreword

The Poverty Reduction and Economic Management Unit in the World Bank's Europe and Central Asia Region has been undertaking a series of analytical works on issues pertinent to the economies in the region. These issues include transition issues; issues of economic integration pertinent for the Central and Eastern Europe countries which are candidates for accession to the European Union; poverty issues; and other economic management issues. The analytical work has been conducted by staff of the unit, other World Bank staff, and specialists outside of the World Bank.

This technical paper series was launched to promote wider dissemination of this analytical work, with the objective of generating further discussion of the issues. The studies published in this series should therefore be viewed as work in progress.

The findings, interpretations, and conclusions are the authors' own and should not be attributed to the World Bank, its Executive Board of Directors, or any of its member countries.

Pradeep Mitra
Director
Poverty Reduction and Economic Management Unit
Europe and Central Asia Region
The World Bank

Abstract

This report was prepared for the World Bank by Peter Havlik, Deputy Director, The Vienna Institute for International Economic Studies (WIIW).

The author wishes to thank M. Landesmann for valuable comments and B. Assenova, R. Prasch, B. Swierczek, and M. Schwarzhappel, all with WIIW, for statistical assistance.

Executive Summary

This study attempts to evaluate various aspects of international competitiveness of the four more developed transition countries in Central and Eastern Europe (the Czech Republic, Hungary, Poland and Slovenia—also called Central and Eastern European Countries, or CEECs), both at the macroeconomic and the industrial branch levels. The cross-country analysis focuses on the evolution of labor cost and trade competitiveness, as well as on the role of exchange rate policies and foreign direct investment (FDI) in the process of catching up and integration with the European Union (EU). Apart from the national statistics available in the WIIW databases, we use also Eurostat data COMEXT database). Based on the research findings, policy recommendations are made for enhancement of international competitiveness in a pre-accession strategy.

Section 1 starts with a review of wage and labor productivity developments, first at the aggregate level of the whole gross domestic product (GDP), then for the manufacturing industry total and for its individual branches at the 2-digit (NACE) level. The newly available data on indirect labor costs allows for a significant expansion of earlier research. Austria is used as a bridge in the cross-country productivity and unit labor cost estimates. Section 2 examines in detail the evolution of export competitiveness as reflected in the changing composition and factor content of manufacturing industry trade with the European Union. It provides some new evidence for emerging trade specialization in the CEECs, identifies industries that are competitive (reflected in market share gains) in the EU, and examines patterns of revealed comparative advantage. Section 3 summarizes the main findings from the ongoing WIIW research on the impact of foreign direct investment on restructuring, and provides also some policy recommendations.

1. Labor Costs and Productivity

Wages: Domestic and International Developments

The four candidate countries for membership in the EU dealt with in this study (the Czech Republic, Hungary, Poland, and Slovenia) represent the most developed transition countries in Europe.[1] Still, their average wages are only a fraction of West European levels, especially when expressed in foreign currency at current exchange rates. According to the most recent data, the average monthly gross wage, converted with current exchange rates, amounted in 1998 to only ECU280–320 in the Czech Republic, Hungary, and Poland. (Note: ECU stands for European Currency Units.) Even in a "high-wage" CEEC such as Slovenia the average monthly gross wage was only ECU850 (table 1). This is much less than in more developed EU countries such as Austria, Germany, France, or the Netherlands (all around ECU2,000). But Slovenian wages are not much lower than wages in either Greece or Portugal, though recent comparable data for the latter two countries are not available. Indirect wage costs are also lower in the CEECs than in the EU, thus magnifying the competitive edge of the CEECs' labor costs.

Wage developments display diverging patterns, not only among the individual transition countries, but also when measured either in domestic or in foreign currency. Initially, the "competitive devaluations" adopted during 1990–91 (except in Hungary) resulted in considerable wage cuts in foreign currency (see figures 1–4). Strong devaluation in the early phase of transition was associated with other reforms, namely, price and trade liberalizations, and with the introduction of current account convertibility. Since about 1992, wages have grown fast in most CEECs, not only thanks to real wage increases measured in domestic currency, but also partly due to the effect of currency appreciation. Excessive currency undervaluation, reflected in initially high exchange rate deviation indices (ERDIs—the ratios between the market exchange rate, exchange rate, and the estimated purchasing power parity, PPP), has been considerably reduced due to subsequent real currency appreciation (especially in the Czech Republic and Poland—see figure 5).[2] The difference between wages converted with the exchange rate on the one hand, and wages converted with the PPP rate on the other hand, thus declined with falling ERDIs, and international wage competitiveness deteriorated for less undervalued currencies. Meanwhile both Hungary and Slovenia pursued a more flexible exchange rate (ER) policy, avoiding large fluctuations in the real ER.

Table 1 Gross Wages and Salaries Per Month Per Employee, Total, European Currency Units at Exchange Rate

	1990	1991	1992	1993	1994	1995	1996	1997	1998	Direct wage costs in percent of total labor costs
Czech Republic[1]	143.6	103.6	126.8	170.5	202.4	238.2	281.1	295.4	323.1	71.3
Slovak Republic	140.0	103.3	124.0	149.5	166.0	187.1	212.3	242.7	252.7	70.8
Hungary[2]	167.1	193.5	218.4	252.8	266.9	239.2	245.0	271.5	281.2	58.9
Poland	85.1	133.8	163.9	184.2	194.8	220.4	258.9	287.6	316.1	69.8
Slovenia[5]	706.9	494.5	486.1	570.2	621.0	731.4	761.8	799.6	848.5	76.0
Bulgaria[4]	378.0	48.9	67.6	99.7	76.8	87.5	75.1	72.4	105.5	72.9
Romania	108.7	97.6	63.7	87.9	92.4	105.8	109.1	104.1	137.3	74.6
Russia	406.9	265.9	18.4	53.0	93.1	90.4	119.1	145.3	99.0	...
Ukraine	335.6	219.8	26.2	32.3	39.8	41.8	59.4	74.0	55.1	...
Austria	1550.4	1648.1	1767.4	1920.5	1995.4	2118.2	2116.4	...	...	49.8
Belgium	1633.6	1756.8	1889.6	2009.9	2164.5	2284.8	...	...	...	52.3
Denmark[5]	2041.9	2123.8	2231.3	2333.9	2420.3	2470.0	...	...	...	80.1
Spain[5]	1598.0	1761.8	1888.2	1793.5	1727.5	1735.2	1827.9	...	...	54.6
Finland	1922.0	1962	1725.4	1498.9	1650.9	1877.6	1913.8	...	...	55.8
France	1496.8	1549.5	1638.4	1738.3	1790.6	1848.4	1904.8	...	...	54.2
Great Britain	1399.4	1538.1	1540.9	1506.7	1576.0	1654.0	...	...	...	74.6
Greece[6]	888.0	944.0	945.0	1004.0	1563.0	...	...	...	...	60.5
Ireland	1862.0	1943.0	2086.0	2029.0	...	...	...	...	...	74.6
Italy	1442.4	1559.0	1582.8	1405.9	1397.0	1307.8	1488.3	...	...	50.3
Netherlands	1799.2	1877.4	2000.5	2159.0	2230.6	2321.1	...	...	...	57.6
Portugal[5][6]	609.4	730.3	866.4	856.5	...	...	...	...	...	55.3
Sweden	1620.8	1713.5	1796.3	1545.5	1624.0	1706.0	...	...	...	58.7
Germany	1613.3	1806.5	1970.0	2029.4	2155.3	2159.1	...	...	...	56.1

... Negligible.

Note: Net wages till 1991 in Poland. Indirect wage costs: 1996 or the latest available year; manufacturing industry.

1. Enterprises with more than 100 employees, in 1992 to 1994 more than 25 employees, from 1997 with more than 20.
2. In 1992, 1993 enterprises with more than 20 employees, from 1994 more than 10, from 1998 more than 5.
3. Up to 1991 excluding private sector.
4. Excluding private sector.
5. Compensation of employees.
6. Non-manual workers in industry.

Source: WIIW estimates based on national statistics, OECD, Eurostat, WIFO and Wirtschaftskammer Österreich (1998).

Real ERs (CPI-based) has appreciated in all CEECs (except Slovenia) during the 1990s. PPI-based real ERs mostly depreciated (except in Poland where there has been a strong real appreciation on both accounts). Despite a clear tendency towards real appreciation, all CEECs maintain a "competitive" exchange rate in terms of high ERDI. The Czech koruna remains more undervalued than the Polish zloty, the Hungarian forint, or the Slovenian tolar (the latter has been the strongest currency in the CEEC region—see figure 5).

Wages in most transition countries are low even when measured at their real purchasing power. The latter is much higher than when judged from nominal wages expressed at ER—in proportion to the ERDI—since most of the local currencies are still grossly undervalued. Taking the PPP-converted wage as a proxy for equilibrium, actual wages (ER converted) in the Czech Republic and Hungary are only around 40 percent of equilibrium wage, in Poland 46 percent, and in Slovenia 67 percent (for 1998—see Annex A). A similar conclusion follows from the International

Figure 1 Wage and Productivity Developments Czech Republic (1989 = 100)

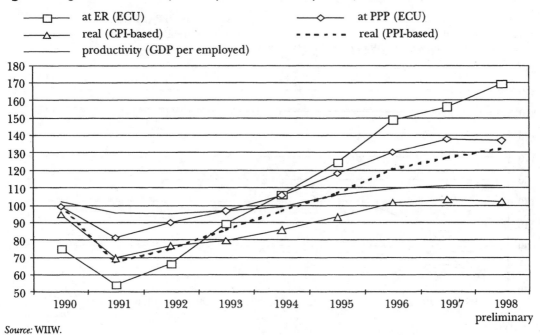

Source: WIIW.

Figure 1 Wage and Productivity Developments Czech Republic (1989 = 100)

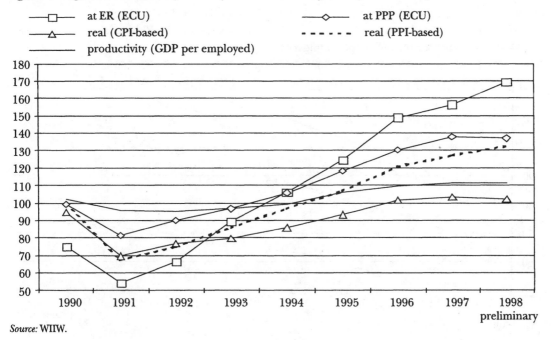

Source: WIIW.

Figure 3 Wage and Productivity Developments Poland (1989 = 100)

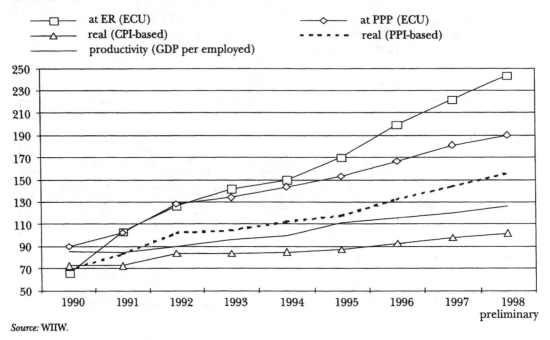

Source: WIIW.

Figure 4 Wage and Productivity Developments Slovenia (1989 = 100)

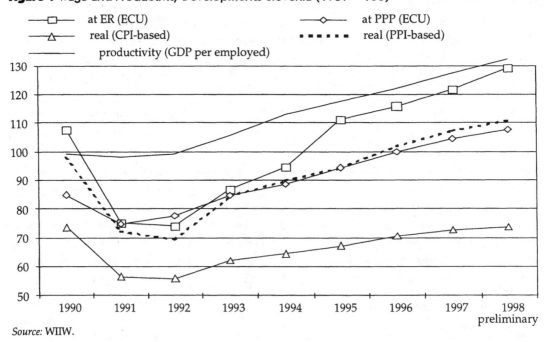

Source: WIIW.

Figure 5 Exchange Rate Deviation Indexes (ERDI = ER/PPP, National Currency Per ECU)

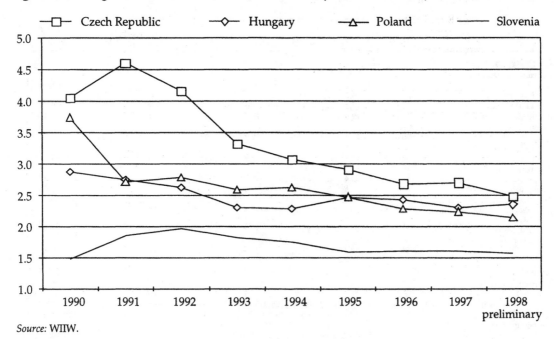

Source: WIIW.

Monetary Fund (IMF) and European Bank for Reconstruction and Development (EBRD) estimates which suggest that actual (U.S. dollar) wages in the Czech Republic, Hungary, and Poland are still considerably below (by 30 to 50 percent) equilibrium.[3] This would imply that in all these countries there is room for additional wage increases and currency appreciation. However, unless accompanied by quality and productivity improvements, a too-strong currency appreciation may lead to current account problems, as the recent experience of Hungary (1995) and the Czech Republic (1997) illustrates.

Similar to movements in the real exchange rate, domestic real wage developments also vary with the price deflator used. In all CEECs, consumer prices increased much more than producer prices during the 1990s (see Annex A). Real product wages (nominal money wages deflated with the producer price index—PPI) have thus been growing faster than real consumer wages (money wages deflated with the consumer price index—CPI), although both indices increased less than those of wages expressed in foreign currency (reflecting effects of currency appreciation—see figures 1–4). Whereas real consumer wages virtually stagnated between 1989 and 1998 (and even declined in Slovenia), real product wages increased considerably everywhere (most in Poland, least in Slovenia). From 1994 to 1998 (after initial price adjustments that led to huge wage fluctuations), real consumer wages grew on annual average by 3.5 percent in Slovenia, 4.1 percent in Poland, and 5.1 percent in the Czech Republic, while in Hungary they declined slightly (table 2). On the other hand, real product wages continued to grow much faster in this period as well: by 8 to 9 percent on annual average in Poland and in the Czech Republic, and by 5.6 percent in Slovenia (in

Table 2 Wages, Productivity, and Unit Labor Costs (ULCs), 1990–1998
(Annual changes in percent)

	1990	1992	1993	1994	1995	1996	1997	1998 prelim.
Czech Republic								
Exchange rate (ER), CZK/ECU	37.9	0.1	−6.9	−0.1	0.7	−0.9	5.3	1.0
Real ER (CPI-based)	31.3	−5.2	−22.0	−7.2	−4.3	−7.0	−1.3	−7.9
Real ER (PPI-based)	38.1	−4.2	−13.7	−3.0	−3.0	−3.4	2.1	−2.8
Average gross wages, CZK	3.7	22.5	25.3	18.5	18.5	18.4	10.5	9.3
Average gross wages, real (PPI-based)	−0.6	11.4	14.7	12.6	10.2	13.1	5.4	4.2
Average gross wages, real (CPI-based)	−5.5	10.2	3.7	7.8	8.6	8.8	1.9	−1.3
Average gross wages, ECU (ER)	−24.8	22.4	34.5	18.7	17.7	19.4	5.0	8.2
Employment total	−1.0	−2.6	−1.6	0.8	2.6	0.7	−1.0	−2.4
GDP per employed person, CZK at 1996 pr.	2.2	−0.7	2.2	2.4	6.8	3.2	1.3	0.1
Unit labor costs, CZK at 1996 prices	1.5	23.4	22.5	15.7	11.0	14.8	9.1	9.2
Unit labor costs, ER (ECU) adjusted	−26.4	23.3	31.6	15.8	10.2	15.8	3.6	8.1
Hungary								
Exchange rate (ER), HUF/ECU	23.7	10.1	5.3	16.1	30.3	17.5	10.3	14.2
Real ER (CPI-based)	0.3	−5.8	−13.0	−0.1	5.4	−3.0	−5.1	0.9
Real ER (PPI-based)	5.9	4.0	−3.8	6.6	4.8	−1.5	−6.7	3.6
Average gross wages, HUF	27.2	24.3	21.9	22.6	16.8	20.4	22.3	18.3
Average gross wages, real (PPI-based)	4.3	11.5	10.0	10.1	−9.4	−1.1	1.6	6.3
Average gross wages, real (CPI-based)	−1.3	1.1	−0.5	3.2	−8.9	−2.6	3.4	3.5
Average gross wages, ECU (ER)	2.8	12.9	15.8	5.6	−10.4	2.5	10.8	3.6
Employment total	−1.9	−19.1	−6.3	−2.0	−1.9	−0.8	0.0	1.4
GDP per employee–person, HUF at 1996 pr.	−1.7	19.8	6.0	5.0	4.5	2.2	4.6	3.6
Unit labor costs, HUF at 1996 prices	29.4	3.8	15.0	16.8	11.7	17.8	16.9	14.2
Unit labor costs, ER (ECU) adjusted	4.6	−5.8	9.2	0.6	−14.3	0.3	5.9	−0.1
Poland								
Exchange rate (ER), PLN/ECU	658.5	34.7	19.9	27.2	16.3	7.7	9.7	5.9
Real ER (CPI-based)	15.6	−0.9	−10.3	−1.6	−5.7	−8.3	−2.8	−4.4
Real ER (PPI-based)	9.7	5.4	−8.0	3.8	−3.9	−2.2	−0.5	−0.4
Average gross wages, PLN	397.9	65.0	34.8	34.5	31.6	26.5	21.9	16.3
Average gross wages, real (PPI-based)	−31.1	22.7	2.1	7.3	4.9	12.6	8.6	8.4
Average gross wages, real (CPI-based)	−27.4	15.4	−0.4	1.7	3.0	5.5	6.1	4.0
Average gross wages, ECU (ER)	−34.4	22.5	12.4	5.7	13.2	17.4	11.1	9.8
Employment total	−4.2	−4.2	−2.4	1.0	1.8	1.9	2.8	0.3
GDP per employee–person, PLN at 1996 pr.	−14.8	7.1	6.3	4.2	11.8	4.0	3.9	4.5
Unit labor costs, PLN at 1996 prices	484.0	54.0	26.7	29.1	17.7	21.7	17.3	11.3
Unit labor costs, ER (ECU) adjusted	−23.0	14.3	5.7	1.5	1.2	12.9	6.9	5.2
Slovenia								
Exchange rate (ER), SIT/ECU	346.0	208.7	26.0	15.2	0.5	10.7	6.4	3.3

(table continued on next page)

Table 2 continued

	1990	1992	1993	1994	1995	1996	1997	1998 prelim.
Real ER (CPI-based)	−28.5	5.7	−4.1	−2.7	−8.2	2.8	−0.1	−3.4
Real ER (PPI-based)	−5.0	2.9	4.9	0.1	−7.7	5.8	2.1	−1.7
Average gross wages, SIT	379.6	203.4	47.8	25.4	18.4	15.3	11.7	9.6
Average gross wages, real (PPI-based)	−2.2	−3.9	21.5	6.6	4.9	8.0	5.3	3.4
Average gross wages, real (CPI-based)	−26.4	−1.3	11.2	3.7	4.3	4.9	3.1	1.6
Average gross wages, ECU (ER)	7.5	−1.7	17.3	8.9	17.8	4.1	5.0	6.1
Employment total	−3.9	−6.5	−3.6	−1.3	−0.1	−0.5	0.2	0.2
GDP per employee-person, SIT at 1996 pr.	−0.9	1.2	6.7	6.7	4.2	4.0	4.4	3.7
Unit labor costs, SIT at 1996 prices	383.8	200.0	38.5	17.6	13.6	10.9	7.1	5.7
Unit labor costs, ER (ECU) adjusted	8.5	−2.8	10.0	2.1	13.0	0.1	0.6	2.3

Source: WIIW estimates based on national statistics, OECD, EUROSTAT and UNIDO.

Hungary only by 1.3 percent). This indicates rapidly rising wage costs for producers which employees (as consumers) did not feel too much in their pockets.

The diverging development of the two price indices (CPI and PPI), and therefore of product and consumer wages, results largely from administered price increases of some nontradables

Figure 6 Unit Labor Costs (ULCs), Exchange Rate (ECU) Adjusted (1989 = 100)

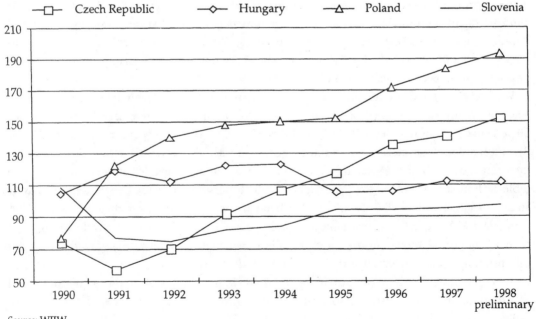

Source: WIIW.

(especially of some services not included in the PPI) and growing workers' demands for wage increases which in turn caused higher wage costs for producers. Moreover, over the whole period (nominal) money wages were growing much faster than labor productivity in all CEECs, indicating rising unit wage costs in domestic currency. Unless compensated for by currency depreciation, rising domestic wage costs resulted also in deteriorating international cost competitiveness. This was the case in all CEECs after 1989, though in Hungary and in Slovenia the growth of wage costs was much less pronounced than in the Czech Republic and Poland (see the developments of international unit labor costs in table 2 and figure 6 and a more detailed discussion below). Preliminary data for 1998 suggest a strong wage increase in the Czech Republic and Poland (close to 10 percent in ECU terms), and moderate wage growth in Slovenia and especially in Hungary (by about 6 percent and 4 percent, respectively). The Czech devaluation (in 1997) and a certain wage restraint (in both 1997 and 1998) helped to reduce somewhat the excessive wage costs growth of the previous years. But these adjustments have so far been much weaker than those applied in Hungary during 1995-96 (see table 2). A recent deterioration of the Polish wage cost competitiveness might require similar policy responses in the near future as well.

In sum, all CEECs maintain a considerable competitive edge due to low wage costs, but the assessment of developments varies widely with the indicator used. Slovenia stands out with nominal wages almost three times as high as in other CEECs, and such a huge wage differential hardly seems to be warranted by correspondingly higher productivity levels (see below). The growth of wages in foreign currency far outstripped domestic wage increases, and real product wages grew much faster than real consumer wages. Such differences may lead not only to widely different analytic and policy conclusions, but also to potentially conflicting reactions of foreign investors, domestic producers, and wage earners. Only in Hungary and in Slovenia, aggregate productivity grew faster than real product wages and wage competitiveness thus improved (figures 2 and 4). On the other hand, productivity growth lagged considerably behind increases in real product wages in the Czech Republic (figure 1) and especially in Poland (figure 3). Whereas in the Czech Republic excessive wage growth was at least halted in 1998, policy corrections aiming at restoring wage competitiveness might soon become necessary in Poland.

Wage levels in the CEEC manufacturing industry are not much different from averages for the whole economy. Gross wages in manufacturing industry ranged between 12 percent to less than 30 percent of the Austrian level in 1997, at PPP rates of 30 percent to 50 percent of that level (table 3). But there are considerable (and mostly growing) wage differences across individual manufacturing industry branches (see figure 7). As shown by the standard deviations of wage levels in table 3, Hungary and Poland show the highest wage dispersion, while the Czech Republic has the smallest wage spread. In all CEECs, there has been an increase in the wage dispersion after 1989. Compared with the manufacturing industry average, wages have been generally declining in the textile, leather, and wood industries, while rapidly growing relative wages are observed in the paper and printing industries, as well as in the chemical industry (figure 7).

In most CEECs, relative wages also increased in the highly successful (and foreign dominated) transport equipment industry—apparently without adversely affecting its competitiveness (see below).

Figure 7 Wage Dispersion (Manufacturing = 100)

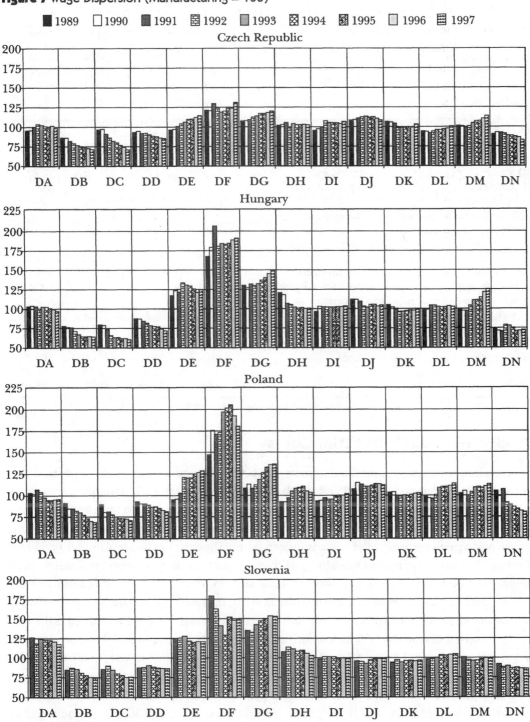

Note: See table 3 for x-axis legend.
Source: WIIW.

Table 3 Monthly Gross Wages in the Manufacturing Industry, 1997
(Manufacturing = 100)

	Czech Republic	Hungary	Poland	Slovenia
Manufacturing total (in ECU, at exchange rate)	287.7	279.3	282.8	659.4
Austria = 100	12.0	11.7	11.8	27.6
Manufacturing total (in ECU, at PPP)	785.7	644.4	629.4	1062.0
Austria = 100	35.0	28.7	28.0	47.3
Manufacturing total = 100				
DA Manufacture of food products; beverages and tobacco	98.3	96.9	95.7	117.4
DB Manufacture of textiles and textile products	71.4	64.0	68.5	74.1
DC Manufacture of leather and leather products	71.1	60.4	70.9	75.6
DD Manufacture of wood and wood products	85.3	71.8	81.2	86.2
DE Manufacture of pulp, paper & paper products; publishing & printing	114.3	124.7	128.7	120.8
DF Manufacture of coke, refined petroleum products & nuclear fuel	130.8	191.0	180.6	149.9
DG Manufacture of chemicals, chemical products and man–made fibers	119.8	149.6	136.2	153.0
DH Manufacture of rubber and plastic products	102.3	100.7	103.4	103.0
DI Manufacture of other non–metallic mineral products	106.7	103.4	102.0	99.6
DJ Manufacture of basic metals and fabricated metal products	108.6	104.8	112.1	99.8
DK Manufacture of machinery and equipment n.e.c.	103.1	98.4	102.8	96.5
DL Manufacture of electrical and optical equipment	100.5	102.5	113.6	104.6
DM Manufacture of transport equipment	113.7	125.3	113.0	99.7
DN Manufacturing n.e.c.	82.9	72.4	80.8	85.7
Standard deviation	16.96	33.96	28.24	23.04

Sources: WIIW estimates based on national statistics, OECD, EUROSTAT and UNIDO.

Productivity and Unit Labor Costs

Low nominal wages, still accentuated in most CEECs by undervalued currencies (see the difference between exchange rate-based and PPP-based wage rates in table 3), have often been treated as these countries' single most important competitive advantage. However, the average productivity in the CEECs is also much lower than in developed market economies, and this productivity gap partly eliminates the cost advantages arising from the low wages. Another part of the low wage cost advantage is eliminated by "quality gaps," related mainly to poorer marketing, packaging, terms of delivery, pre- and after-sale services, and so forth.[4] Low wages thus cannot be treated separately from labor productivity since the latter is, in general, also fairly low in the CEECs. What really matters in terms of wage competitiveness are *unit labor costs (ULCs)*, defined as the ratio of wage costs to labor productivity. Below, we shall attempt to derive consistent ULC estimates, starting with the analysis of ULC trends and then moving on to more difficult level comparisons. On an aggregate basis, we use the above-quoted data on average gross wages (plus the available information on indirect wage costs); the aggregate productivity is approximated by the GDP per employed person at constant (1996) prices. Furthermore, the ULCs have to be adjusted for changes in the exchange rate for purposes of international comparisons.[5]

Let us first examine productivity and ULC developments over time, which do not require complicated productivity level comparisons (we assume also that the indirect wage cost component remained constant during the period). After 1992, there were impressive improvements of aggregate productivity in Hungary, Poland, and Slovenia, whereas productivity growth was sluggish in the Czech Republic (table 2, figures 1–4). As mentioned above, however, productivity growth frequently lagged behind wage increases in other countries as well, indicating declining labor cost competitiveness. Aggregate ULCs (ECU adjusted) rose during the 1990s, especially in Poland and the Czech Republic; for example, productivity lagged considerably behind the growth of nominal ECU wages, whereas ULC growth was much less pronounced in Hungary and Slovenia (part of ULC growth resulted also from appreciating currencies—see figure 6). Table 2 shows that in the period 1994–98 labor cost competitiveness deteriorated in the Czech Republic (ECU-adjusted ULCs grew by 11 percent on average during 1994–98), Poland (7 percent), and Slovenia (4 percent), while it has markedly improved with declining ULCs in Hungary.

In the manufacturing industry (data are available until 1997 only), international ULCs have been growing less rapidly than in the economy as a whole (in the Czech Republic, Poland, and Slovenia), or the ULC's drop in manufacturing was much more pronounced (in Hungary, for example) than in the whole economy. This drop resulted from a generally faster growth of productivity in the manufacturing industry. Again, developments are extremely uneven across countries and individual branches of the industry (figure 8). An outstanding feature has been impressive ULC improvements in almost all branches of Hungarian manufacturing after 1992 (ULC in the Hungarian manufacturing industry dropped by 7 percent per year during 1993–97), sharply contrasting with the deteriorating labor cost competitiveness of most industries in the Czech Republic and Poland, at least until 1996 (see figure 8 and detailed data in Annex B). A startling feature is the remarkable ULC improvements (mainly thanks to huge productivity increases) in transport equipment, electrical, and optical equipment industries, highly penetrated by FDI in all CEECs. This provides another piece of clear evidence for efficiency gains brought about by foreign management (see below).

A comparison of ULC *levels* across countries requires *internationally comparable productivity level estimates* in order to eliminate not only exchange rate fluctuations, but also cross-country differences in the base year price level. There is hardly any literature regarding ULC level estimates for the transition countries.[6] The main problem is certainly posed by the lack of comparable productivity statistics, but reliable data on total wage costs are also difficult to obtain. Hitchens and others (1995) have compared productivity and wages in a sample of manufacturing plants in the Czech Republic and Hungary with that of Germany (separately for East and West Germany). Their sample results show that in 1993 the Czech manufacturing productivity was 18 percent (and the Hungarian 20 percent) of the 1988 West German level when estimated from the value added. Physical productivity was much higher than value-added productivity: 30 percent of the West German level in the Czech Republic and 44 percent of that level in Hungary. These productivity estimates would tentatively imply manufacturing ULCs ranging from 21 percent to 35 percent of the West German level for the Czech Republic and between 24 percent and 53 percent of the West German level for Hungary. (The lower range is for physical productivity estimates; wage data refer

11

Figure 8 Unit Labor Costs (European Currency Unit–Adjusted), Annual Growth Rates in Percent

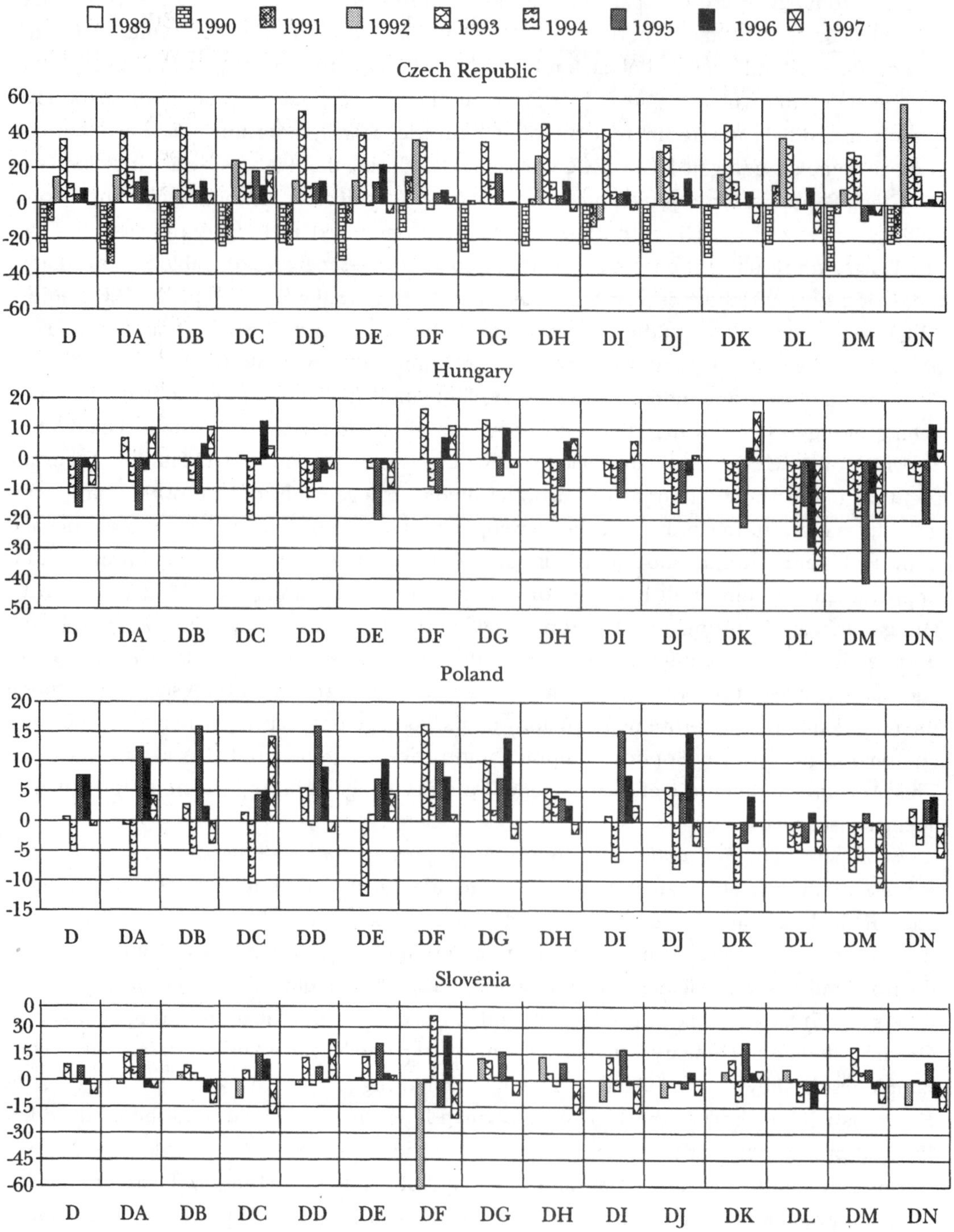
1989
1990
1991
1992
1993
1994
1995
1996
1997
Czech Republic
Hungary
Poland
Slovenia
D DA DB DC DD DE DF DG DH DI DJ DK DL DM DN

Note: See table 3 for x-axis legend.
Source: WIIW.

to gross wages and not to total wage costs.) Another recent source uses the same approach for productivity estimates as the present study (GDP per employed person at PPPs), but provides data on total wage costs, though only for the Czech Republic and other selected OECD countries in the year 1993. The aggregate Czech ULCs were estimated at 23 percent of the West German and Austrian levels in 1993 (Fassman 1996).

Generally, international productivity comparisons are problematic even for Western market economies. At the aggregate level of the whole economy, one can use real GDP per employed person as a crude proxy for cross-country productivity comparison, where the GDP is converted from national currency with the help of purchasing power parities (PPPs) in order to approximate internationally comparable price levels.

This adjustment is of particular importance for transition countries where exchange rates are grossly misleading, owing to their still undervalued and widely fluctuating currencies (see above). On this crude basis, the 1996 aggregate productivity level (real GDP per employed person at PPPs) in Central and Eastern Europe was highest in Slovenia (about 60 percent of the average Austrian and EU level; the latter is estimated at approximately ECU46,000—48,000 in 1996), followed by the Czech Republic, Hungary (both about 50 percent of the EU level) and Poland (36 percent— see table 4). The CEECs' estimated productivity gap is thus considerably smaller than their relative wage gaps with respect to developed market economies of Western Europe.

Table 4 Central and Eastern European Aggregate Wages, Productivity and Unit Labor
Costs in 1996
(Austria = 100)

	Wages (gross)		
	ER based	PPP based	ER, including indirect costs
Czech Republic	13.3	39.5	13.3
Hungary	11.4	30.8	14.1
Poland	12.1	30.6	12.3
Slovenia	35.5	63.5	33.3
	Productivity (GDP/employed)		
	ER based	PPP based	ERDI
Czech Republic	17.0	51.2	2.71
Hungary	18.5	50.0	2.43
Poland	14.3	36.1	2.28
Slovenia	38.1	68.9	1.63
	ULCs (ER–based wage/productivity)		
	ER based	PPP based	PPP, including indirect costs
Czech Republic	78.1	25.9	25.9
Hungary	61.6	22.8	28.1
Poland	84.7	33.4	34.1
Slovenia	93.2	51.6	48.3

Note: Austrian direct wage costs (71.2 percent of total labor costs) include 13. and 14. salary.
Source: WIIW estimates based on national statistics, WIFO, Wirtschaftskammer Österreich and OECD.

The comparison of ULC levels across countries can again use the above-quoted PPP-converted GDP per employed person as proxies for comparable productivity levels, and to compare the level of the CEECs' ULC with Austria.[7] At the aggregate level (and first without taking into account indirect wage costs), our estimates show that the CEECs' ULC ranged between 25 percent (Hungary and the Czech Republic) and 60 percent (Slovenia) of the Austrian level in 1996. Including indirect labor costs, the gap becomes somewhat smaller for Hungary (total ULCs were 28 percent of the Austrian level) but somewhat larger for Slovenia (54 percent).[8] A projection of benchmark ULC level estimates into the wage and productivity trends presented above shows that, despite considerable increases during 1990–98 in most CEECs, even in "high-wage" Slovenia average PPP-based ULCs were only around 60 percent of the Austrian level in 1998 (about 50 percent with indirect wage costs included)., Slovenia was followed, after a large gap, by Poland (40 percent), the Czech Republic (30 percent) and Hungary (26 percent) (see figure 9 and Annex A).

Figure 9 International Comparison of Unit Labor Costs (ULCs), PPP Adjusted (Austria = 100)

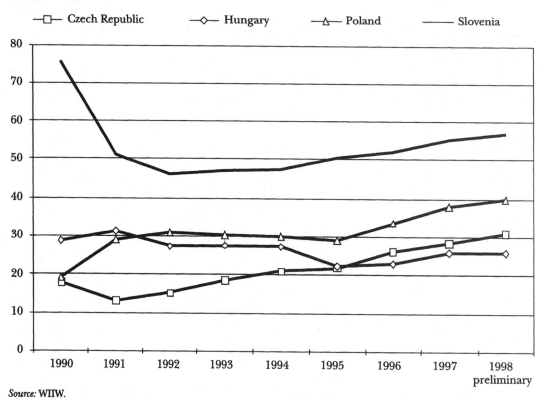

Source: WIIW.

Productivity and Unit Labor Costs Levels in Manufacturing Industry

As mentioned above, we get a similar general picture of ULC developments when we look at industry, though data comparability problems (especially regarding productivity measurement) are here even more formidable than for the whole economy (table 5).[9] In most CEECs, industrial ULC grew less strongly than in the economy as a whole, largely due to much more pronounced productivity improvements in this sector. Global trends in both ULC indicators are roughly the same: until very recently, we find rising ULC in the Czech Republic and Poland (and hence deteriorating cost competitiveness) but only moderate ULC growth in Hungary and even less in Slovenia. At this stage of research there is still no information on the comparative level of domestic prices in the CEEC's manufacturing industry, which would be required for genuine international productivity and ULC-level comparisons.

Assuming that relative price levels in the manufacturing industry (and more ambitiously, in its individual branches) are roughly the same as over the whole GDP, one could make the same (crude) comparison of relative ULC levels across the manufacturing industry branches with the help of the above PPP estimates. This is of course a great simplification. In fact, even detailed PPP calculations show large differences in the price levels across individual GDP components. In all CEECs, for instance, the price level of gross fixed capital formation, especially of machinery and equipment, was much higher (by about 20–50 percent) than the price level over the whole GDP; this results mainly from the high share of imported machinery and equipment in investment outlays.[10] Since we would really need for our purposes at least the price relations of domestically produced machinery and equipment, our estimates of manufacturing industry productivity in the CEECs using PPPs for the whole GDP are probably overestimated, and those of ULC underestimated. We shall also show alternative productivity and ULC estimates below, using partial PPPs (which yield lower productivity estimates) for gross fixed capital formation.[11]

The estimated productivity in the CEECs' manufacturing industry ranges between one third and one half of the Austrian level, depending on the price level indicator used (table 6). An interesting finding is the good productivity performance of Hungary's manufacturing industry (better than in the Czech Republic) and a relatively poor standing for Slovenia, at least in terms of productivity measured at PPP for GDP. In contrast with wages, Slovenia's labor productivity at PPP

Table 5 Unit Labor Costs (ULCs) in Industry (Wages/Productivity), Exchange Rate (ECU) Adjusted (Change in percent against preceding year)

	1990	1991	1992	1993	1994	1995	1996	1997	1998 prelim.
Czech Republic	−25.1	−14.9	23.7	33.3	11.4	6.2	8.0	−2.6	5.1
Hungary	4.6	18.2	20.1	4.6	−9.6	−15.8	−5.3	−3.0	−8.9
Poland	−23.0	55.8	−9.5	4.8	−2.7	5.3	7.0	−1.7	2.6
Slovenia	11.5	−28.0	−1.3	8.9	−2.5	9.7	−5.7	0.9	1.9

Source: National statistics; WIIW estimate.

for gross fixed capital formation (PPPCAP) seems to be only marginally higher than in other CEECs.[12] Another interesting finding is that manufacturing industry labor productivity levels in these four more developed CEECs are roughly the same. Estimates from data on 2-digit NACE industries indicate much larger productivity than wage differences across individual manufacturing branches.[13] In the Czech Republic in 1997, for example, manufacturing industry wages varied between 71 percent of the manufacturing industry average in the textiles and textile products industry and 130 percent of the manufacturing average in the coke, petroleum, and nuclear fuels industry. In contrast, labor productivity ranged from 50 percent of the average in the textiles and textile products industries to almost 400 percent of the average in the capital-intensive coke and petroleum industry. An even larger dispersion of manufacturing industry labor productivity can be observed in Poland and in Slovenia. Compared to Austria, productivity levels are relatively high in the Czech Republic's and Slovenia's food and beverage industry, pulp and paper industry (also in Poland), chemicals, and rubber and plastic products. On the other hand, textiles, leather, and machinery and equipment n.e.c. all have rather poor productivity performance (table 6). Nevertheless, the evaluation of comparative productivity levels certainly merits further research.

Table 6 Productivity in the Manufacturing Industry, 1996
(Manufacturing = 100)

	Czech Republic	Hungary	Poland	Slovenia
Manufacturing total, productivity in ECU				
(at PPP96 for GDP)	71782	76900	58884	69917
Austria = 100	53.0	56.8	43.5	51.7
Manufacturing total, productivity in ECU				
(at PPPCAP96)	48628	48877	44705	59692
Austria = 100	35.2	35.4	32.3	43.2
Manufacturing total = 100				
DA Manufacture of food products; beverages and tobacco	170.3	131.7	142.2	182.3
DB Manufacture of textiles and textile products	49.9	28.2	40.1	44.8
DC Manufacture of leather and leather products	52.2	24.5	49.7	51.2
DD Manufacture of wood and wood products	78.8	65.8	83.6	77.9
DE Manufacture of pulp, paper and paper products; publishing and printing	128.1	105.3	148.3	114.1
DF Manufacture of coke, refined petroleum products, and nuclear fuel	378.4	288.6	558.6	541.9
DG Manufacture of chemicals, chemical products, and man-made fibers	188.7	146.6	152.7	194.9
DH Manufacture of rubber and plastic products	98.5	114.5	115.4	107.4
DI Manufacture of other non-metallic mineral products	86.8	75.7	79.2	85.0
DJ Manufacture of basic metals and fabricated metal products	97.2	105.8	103.5	87.1
DK Manufacture of machinery and equipment n.e.c.	57.0	68.6	67.7	87.8
DL Manufacture of electrical and optical equipment	66.3	98.7	97.8	78.6
DM Manufacture of transport equipment	132.8	195.5	106.4	178.6
DN Manufacturing n.e.c.	61.9	43.1	71.3	87.4
Standard deviation	83.52	67.81	123.57	121.11

Source: WIIW estimates based on national statistics, OECD, EUROSTAT and UNIDO.

Recently available information on total and indirect labor costs in manufacturing industry branches of selected CEECs (Czech Republic, Hungary, and Poland—see Annex B) allow us to estimate not only wage costs but total ULC as well. Relating the total labor costs data to the above alternative productivity estimates, we get a tentative picture for *ranges in sectoral ULC levels* in the manufacturing industry, again relative to Austria. The lower ULC range results from (higher) labor productivity estimates obtained with conversion using PPP for the whole GDP (table 7a), the upper range from (lower) labor productivity estimates when using PPPs for gross fixed capital formation (PPPCAP—table 7b).[14]

An overview of the main findings is presented below:

- As expected, the highest total ULCs in the manufacturing industry were registered in Slovenia—about 46 percent of the Austrian level in 1996 (or, alternatively, more than 55 percent if the PPP for gross fixed capital formation. PPPCAP, is taken as a yardstick for a comparable price level), followed by Poland and Hungary with 22 to 24 percent (33 to 36 percent for PPPCAP) and the Czech Republic with 21 percent (31 percent for PPPCAP). Slovenia's ULCs were thus about twice as high as in the remaining CEECs.
- In a sectoral perspective and relative to Austria, the highest ULCs are recorded in the leather and textiles industries in Hungary and Slovenia (coke, petroleum, and nuclear fuel is an outlier). Using PPPCAP, Hungarian ULC in the leather industry were very close to the Austrian level and the labor cost competitiveness (as in textiles) was therefore minimal. In Poland, the highest ULC are also observed in the textiles and leather industries (close to 40-50 percent of the Austrian level). In the Czech Republic, ULC were highest in the leather industry and in machinery and equipment n.e.c. (about 30 percent of the Austrian level, or close to 50 percent with PPPCAP productivity conversion), followed by textiles and electrical and optical equipment.
- The Czech Republic had in 1996 the lowest ULC in manufacturing industry, but not in all branches: in rubber and plastic products, basic metals and fabricated metal products, machinery and equipment, electrical and optical equipment, as well as in transport equipment industry, the Czech ULC were higher than in Hungary, and in some cases even higher than in Poland. Frequently, these are industries characterized by an extremely high foreign ownership penetration and huge productivity improvements in recent years. Hungary's lead in foreign penetration thus shows up in its competitive edge.

In the Czech Republic, the international (measured in ECU) ULC in the manufacturing industry grew rapidly until 1996, due to both sluggish productivity growth and rapid wage increases, which were both magnified by currency appreciations (see Annex B for separate developments of wages and labor productivity by industries). In contrast, Hungarian and Polish manufacturing industry productivity was growing fast: about 15 percent per year between 1993and 1997 in the case of Hungary, and somewhat less in the case of Poland. As a result, Hungarian international manufacturing industry ULC dropped by more than 30 percent between 1993 and 1997; Polish data suggest an increase by about 7 percent per year after 1995 (with a minor decline in 1997). A

Table 7a International Comparison of Total Labor Costs in the Manufacturing Industry
(1996, PPP for GDP, Austria = 100)

	Czech Republic	Hungary	Poland	Slovenia[1]
D Manufacturing	20.7	22.3	24.3	46.3
DA Manufacture of food products; beverages and tobacco	15.4	20.7	20.2	38.2
DB Manufacture of textiles and textile products	27.0	44.7	38.0	71.0
DC Manufacture of leather and leather products	31.3	57.7	38.3	73.8
DD Manufacture of wood and wood products	23.7	26.7	25.7	54.9
DE Manufacture of pulp, paper and paper products; publishing and printing	19.0	27.2	21.8	51.8
DF Manufacture of coke, refined petroleum products, and nuclear fuel	31.9	74.6	39.3	58.6
DG Manufacture of chemicals, chemical products and man-made fibers	14.9	25.6	24.0	41.2
DH Manufacture of rubber and plastic products	19.0	17.0	19.2	40.4
DI Manufacture of other non-metallic mineral products	21.4	25.6	26.6	46.1
DJ Manufacture of basic metals and fabricated metal products	20.7	19.3	24.0	46.4
DK Manufacture of machinery and equipment n.e.c.	28.7	25.7	29.3	40.6
DL Manufacture of electrical and optical equipment	24.8	19.0	22.2	50.2
DM Manufacture of transport equipment	22.6	17.8	33.4	33.8
DN Manufacturing n.e.c.	24.1	30.2	23.3	38.2

Table 7b International Comparison of Total Labor Costs in the Manufacturing Industry
(1996, PPP for Gross Fixed Capital Formation, Austria = 100)

	Czech Republic	Hungary	Poland	Slovenia[1]
D Manufacturing	31.2	35.8	32.7	55.4
DA Manufacture of food products; beverages and tobacco	23.3	33.3	27.1	45.7
DB Manufacture of textiles and textile products	40.8	71.9	51.1	85.0
DC Manufacture of leather and leather products	47.2	92.7	51.6	88.3
DD Manufacture of wood and wood products	35.7	42.9	34.6	65.7
DE Manufacture of pulp, paper and paper products; publishing and printing	28.6	43.7	29.4	62.0
DF Manufacture of coke, refined petroleum products, and nuclear fuel	48.1	119.9	52.9	70.1
DG Manufacture of chemicals, chemical products and man-made fibers	22.5	41.2	32.3	49.3
DH Manufacture of rubber and plastic products	28.7	27.4	25.9	48.3
DI Manufacture of other non-metallic mineral products	32.3	41.1	35.7	55.2
DJ Manufacture of basic metals and fabricated metal products	31.3	31.0	32.3	55.5
DK Manufacture of machinery and equipment n.e.c.	43.4	41.3	39.5	48.6
DL Manufacture of electrical and optical equipment	37.5	30.6	29.8	60.0
DM Manufacture of transport equipment	34.2	28.5	45.0	40.4
DN Manufacturing n.e.c.	36.4	48.5	31.4	45.8

Note: 1. Indirect labor costs estimated as 24 percent of total labor costs for all branches.
Sources: WIIW estimates based on national statistics, Wirtschaftskammer Österreichs, OECD, EUROSTAT and United Nations Industrial Development Organization (UNIDO).

more intensive involvement of foreign investors in the Hungarian manufacturing industry brought about large efficiency gains, visible also in the improved labor costs competitiveness, during recent years. Hungarian labor cost competitiveness in manufacturing industry improved markedly, and in several branches ULCs had dropped below the level of the Czech Republic and Poland by 1996. The growth of Slovenian manufacturing industry ULCs has been modest (about 3 percent per year on average during 1993–97), but their level is still about twice as high as in the remaining three CEECs.

Excessive wage growth and currency appreciation, which is not accompanied either by corresponding productivity improvements or compensated by improved quality, leads to a deterioration of cost competitiveness. This deterioration may cause external disequilibrium that requires painful policy adjustments. Such a situation occurred in Hungary in 1995 and in the Czech Republic in 1997. Recent developments of labor competitiveness and deteriorating current accounts indicate that Poland could become vulnerable soon as well. On the other hand, Slovenia stands out as a permanently high-costs country among other CEECs—so far without encountering any serious difficulties with maintaining external equilibrium.

In sum, all CEECs still maintain a considerable, though mostly diminishing, competitive edge over Western Europe due to low wage costs, but the assessment varies with the indicator used, and the situation rapidly changes. Such differences may lead not only to varying analytical and policy conclusions, but potentially to conflicts between foreign investors, domestic producers, and wage earners, as each of them may look at the situation from a different angle. Our analysis has shown that low unit labor costs, averaging less than one third of the West European level (30–40 percent of the Austrian level in 1998) in all CEECs except Slovenia (here about 60 percent of the Austrian level), together with the geographic proximity to Western markets and a fairly good formal qualification of the labor force, give the CEECs an important competitive edge. This is true not only for traditional labor-intensive industries (in fact, the labor cost advantages of labor-intensive industries seem to be least pronounced), but with progress in the transition, more FDI, and restructuring, especially for other more sophisticated industry branches like transport, electrical, and optical equipment. As shown in Section 2 below, mainly the latter branches have been highly successful in exports. Moreover, the above crude ULC estimates for manufacturing industry are sectoral averages that presumably vary considerably across companies, especially with respect to productivity levels. Numerous examples can be increasingly found where Western management, quality control standards, and marketing channels help to substantially raise the average productivity levels while still maintaining considerable wage gaps (for example, in the transport equipment, electrotechnical, and chemical industries).

2. Trade Specialization and Competitiveness of Manufacturing Industry

Central and Eastern European Countries' Competitive Export Industries

This section attempts to evaluate the export competitiveness and emerging patterns of trade specialization as reflected in the evolving structure and factor content of the CEECs' manufacturing industry trade with the European Union—that is, the EU(12).[15] After reviewing aggregate manufacturing industry trade performance, we undertake a detailed analysis of market shares in order to identify CEEC industries that are increasingly competitive in the EU market. We then calculate revealed comparative advantage (RCA) values and examine the factor content of these industries in order to detect emerging patterns of trade specialization. The analysis focuses mainly on the period 1993–97, when the initial transformation recession was already largely overcome and most CEECs had embarked on a growth path. Using the detailed Eurostat COMEXT database (at NACE 3-digit level, more than 100 industries), we provide some updated and new, though still preliminary, evidence for emerging trade specialization patterns and the export competitiveness of manufacturing industries in the CEECs.

Traditional trade theories suggest that each country will export goods that are intensive in its relatively abundant factor input (the Heckscher-Ohlin theory), or that the trade structure results from comparative advantages in productivity (Ricardo). Many assumptions of these traditional trade theories are clearly not fulfilled (especially in the case of the transition countries), but even new trade theories leave some scope for the importance of factor endowment. We do not aspire to provide a proper test of different trade theories, but would expect to find distinct patterns of trade specialization since the development level of the CEECs is far below the EU average. In fact, the labor cost advantages described above would theoretically give the CEECs an important competitive edge in labor-intensive industries. On the other hand, there is still a shortage of capital and the skills required for a market economy in most CEECs; this can be in some cases alleviated by inflows of FDI. All this has an impact on the structure of CEECs' trade flows. Differences among the individual CEECs, confirmed by earlier studies, emerge as well.

The CEECs' manufacturing industry exports to the EU(12) have grown almost five fold since 1989; between 1993 and 1997 they almost doubled in ECU terms. The CEEC(4) (the Czech Republic, Hungary, Poland, and Slovenia) combined market share in the EU(12) manufacturing imports, discounting intra-EU trade, reached 6 percent in 1997, compared to only 2 percent in 1989 and 4.4 percent in 1993 (the former year without Slovenia, see tables 8 and 9). But the CEECs manufacturing industry imports from the EU(12) have been growing even faster: they have increased more than five times since 1989 and by more than 120 percent from 1993 to 1997. The trade deficit with the EU(12) has been growing and reached ECU13.9 billion in 1997 (tables 10 through 12). The trade liberalization measures entailed in the Association Agreements thus led to a significant trade expansion in both the EU and the CEECs. Judging from the highly positive and growing trade balance, exporters from the EU(12) have successfully penetrated CEEC markets —despite the asymmetric trade liberalization in favor of the CEECs. Another feature of EU–CEEC trade is a huge discrepancy in the importance of each of the respective markets: the EU absorbs 60 percent (the Czech Republic) to 76 percent (Slovenia) of CEEC exports, whereas only about 7 percent of EU(12) exports (or about 2 percent if intra-EU trade is included) are destined for the CEECs.

We start with an analysis of the changes in the market shares in the EU(12) and identify the CEECs' most competitive and important export industries (that is, industries with the biggest absolute market share gains). Needless to say, the period for which detailed trade data are available has been not only very short, but also rather turbulent for providing firm evidence for the CEECs' long-term comparative advantages. Until 1993, most CEEC economies were in a deep transformational recession resulting from the combined effect of systemic changes and the loss of traditional Council of Mutual Economic Assistance (CMEA) markets.[16] Industrial recovery started first in Poland in 1992, followed by Hungary in 1993. Developments have been highly uneven, both across countries and individual industries; some CEECs (the Czech Republic in particular) have recently even contracted again. As shown above in section 1 of this paper, a new feature of the recent industrial development in the region has been fairly high labor productivity increases, especially in Poland and Hungary (less so in the Czech Republic and in Slovenia) and in branches of industry with high FDI penetration. The combined effect of wage, exchange rate, and productivity developments frequently resulted in rising, though in international comparison still extremely low, labor costs.

A detailed "shift and share" market analysis reveals that about 70 percent of the CEECs' 1993–97 export increment (of more than ECU17 billion) can be attributed to "competitive gains" of market shares in the EU, whereas the effect of "general demand growth" was much smaller (less than 30 percent of the total export increment) and the "structural effect" was actually negative.[17] The largest competitive gains were recorded in a heterogeneous mix of industries, but unlike the initial period of "passive restructuring" (roughly until 1993), a larger number of more sophisticated branches of industry has now become prominent: motor vehicles (NACE 351), electrical machinery (342), tools and finished metal goods (316), radio and TV sets (345), and parts and accessories for motor vehicles (353) all recorded the largest competitive gains (for data by individual CEECs see Annex C). In some of these industries, the CEECs' market shares in the extra-

Table 8 European Union(12)—Manufacturing Industry Imports from Central and Eastern European Countries, European Currency Unit Millions
(Without intra-EU trade)

	1989	1990	1991	1992	1993	1994	1995	1996	1997
Czech Republic	—	—	—	—	4430.7	5888.5	7410	7983.7	9691.8
Hungary	2181.8	2547.1	3138.0	3553.8	3525.3	4412.8	5951.5	6608.3	8984.9
Poland	2842.0	3961.9	4973.4	5983.8	6578.0	7935.8	10076.2	10205.9	11897.9
Slovenia	—	—	—	—	2809.7	3358.9	3738	3685.1	3961.4
CEEC(4)	—	—	—	—	**17343.6**	**21596.0**	**27175.7**	**28483.0**	**34535.9**
EU total	**336526.4**	**343410.8**	**374619.6**	**377763.1**	**391256.4**	**439193.7**	**475883.6**	**495125.3**	**578146.1**

— Not available.
Source: Eurostat COMEXT database, own calculations.

Table 9 Central and Eastern European Countries' Market Shares in the European Union(12) Manufacturing Industry Imports
(Without intra–EU trade)

	1989	1990	1991	1992	1993	1994	1995	1996	1997
Czech Republic	—	—	—	—	1.13	1.34	1.56	1.61	1.68
Hungary	0.65	0.74	0.84	0.94	0.90	1.00	1.25	1.33	1.55
Poland	0.84	1.15	1.33	1.58	1.68	1.81	2.12	2.06	2.06
Slovenia	—	—	—	—	0.72	0.76	0.79	0.74	0.69
CEEC(4)	—	—	—	—	**4.43**	**4.92**	**5.71**	**5.75**	**5.97**

— Not available.
Source: Eurostat COMEXT database, own calculations.

Table 10 European Union(12)—Manufacturing Industry Exports to Central and Eastern European Countries, European Currency Unit Millions
(Without intra–EU trade)

	1989	1990	1991	1992	1993	1994	1995	1996	1997
Czech Republic	—	—	—	—	5625.0	7382.6	9492.5	11439.0	12917.5
Hungary	2673.0	2623.7	3136.4	3745.1	4594.3	5711.1	6390.6	7396.5	10108.1
Poland	3299.4	3716.8	6662.8	6967.2	8677.8	9815.7	12418.2	16063.9	20501.8
Slovenia	—	—	—	—	2859.5	3391.6	4076	4229.9	4900.2
CEEC(4)	—	—	—	—	21756.6	26301.0	32377.3	39129.2	48427.7
EU total	**368955.5**	**370080.6**	**380934.2**	**394371.3**	**451697.3**	**502771.9**	**553162.5**	**602092.4**	**691524.4**

— Not available.
Source: Eurostat COMEXT database, own calculations.

EU(12) imports are remarkably high. The industries listed above have enjoyed the biggest absolute market share gains in most CEECs, either over the whole period from 1989 to 1997, or, after incurring initial losses at the beginning of the transition, consolidating their exports from 1993 on and winning market shares afterwards. On the other hand, some industries have incurred "competitive losses," again either over the whole period from 1989 to 1997 or, suffering from a sort of adverse restructuring effect, only after 1993. Clear losers over the whole period were parts of the food pro-

Table 11 Central and Eastern European Countries' Shares in European Union(12) Manufacturing Industry Exports
(Without intra–EU trade)

	1989	1990	1991	1992	1993	1994	1995	1996	1997
Czech Republic	—	—	—	—	1.25	1.47	1.72	1.90	1.87
Hungary	0.72	0.71	0.82	0.95	1.02	1.14	1.16	1.23	1.46
Poland	0.89	1.00	1.75	1.77	1.92	1.95	2.24	2.67	2.96
Slovenia	—	—	—	—	0.63	0.67	0.74	0.70	0.71
CEEC(4)	—	—	—	—	**4.82**	**5.23**	**5.85**	**6.50**	**7.00**

— Not available.
Source: Eurostat COMEXT database, own calculations.

Table 12 CEECs' Trade Balances in Manufacturing Industry Trade with the European Union(12), European Currency Unit Millions

	1989	1990	1991	1992	1993	1994	1995	1996	1997
Czech Republic	—	—	—	—	–1194.3	–1494.1	–2082.5	–3455.3	–3225.7
Hungary	–491.2	–76.6	1.6	–191.3	–1069.0	–1298.3	–439.1	–788.2	–1123.3
Poland	–457.4	245.1	–1689.4	–983.4	–2099.8	–1879.9	–2342.0	–5858.0	–8603.9
Slovenia	—	—	—	—	–49.8	–32.7	–338.0	–544.7	–938.8
CEEC(4)	—	—	—	—	**–4413.0**	**–4705.0**	**–5201.6**	**–10646.2**	**–13891.8**

— Not available.
Source: Eurostat COMEXT database, own calculations.

cessing industry (such as fruit and vegetables and fish and meat processing) in Hungary and Poland. This is largely due to the still existing EU trade barriers in the agro-food trade. But more recently (1993–97), competitive losses are being recorded also in clothing, footwear, and furniture (as well as building materials and cement in the Czech Republic)—all industries which were viewed as highly competitive in the period before 1993 (Havlik 1995). Contrary to the past, the latest analysis thus reveals new, distinct patterns of trade competitiveness and restructuring.

Emerging Specialization Patterns of Central and Eastern European Countries' Exports

Several earlier studies (for example, Sheehy 1995, Dobrinsky and Landesmann 1995) have discerned general specialization effects of the CEECs' exports on Western markets, most notably, a move away from exports from energy- and capital-intensive branches of industry towards labor-intensive industries. Sheehy (1995) noted the high concentration of CEEC exports in clothing and footwear, metals, chemicals, wooden furniture, and timber in the initial transition period. Landesmann (1995) analyzed the factor content of CEEC exports to the EU during 1989–93 and compared the export shares of these industries with the representation of the same industries in total EU imports by looking at the 10, 20, and 30 most x-factor-intensive exports out of about 90 NACE categories for which factor intensities are available. At the beginning of the 1990s, there was an over-representation of labor- and energy-intensive industries in the CEECs' exports to the EU and a huge gap in the representation of skill- and R&D-intensive industries. The latter gaps have somewhat narrowed in Hungary and Czechoslovakia, but not so much in Poland, whereas they remained practically unchanged in other CEECs (Bulgaria and Romania). Dobrinsky (1995) noted that an excessive specialization of the CEECs on energy-intensive industries was not economically viable because it resulted from the access to cheap energy in the past. On the other hand, Aiginger and others. (1994) have found little evidence for factor intensities as an explanation of the 1988–92 bilateral trade flows between Austria and selected CEECs.

We now analyze the factor content of the CEEC export industries in the more recent period (1993–97) and look first at the characteristics of the most competitive sectors. Can we find new, distinct (or changing) specialization patterns apart from the general features observed in the first phase of transition described earlier? As mentioned above, for example, clothing and knitting industries—both among the most labor-intensive sectors with relatively high ULC—have been suffering from competitive losses in the recent period. On the other hand, the highly R&D- and skill-intensive electrical machinery industry gained a lot, especially in Czech and Hungarian exports to the EU. In the early phase of transition, some highly capital- and energy-intensive industries, such as the iron and steel and cement industries, also enjoyed competitive gains (Havlik 1995). Specialization patterns are thus complex and changing, despite a general theoretical expectation of CEEC competitive advantage in labor-intensive industries on the one hand, and the under-representation of capital-, skill- and R&D-intensive industries in exports to the EU on the other hand. Besides, there are again considerable differences among the individual CEECs.

We look first at the characteristics of the sample of the 50 most competitive CEEC industries identified by the above "shift and share" analysis for the period 1993–97. We shall compare the average x-factor content of these industries with the average for all 92 industries for which x-factor intensities are available.[18] As expected, the pattern is uneven across countries and changes over time, reflecting different speeds in industrial and export restructuring: during the earlier period, the most competitive industries (that is, industries with the largest absolute market share gains in 1993–95) in all CEECs displayed a higher than average labor intensity and lower than average capital intensity (see Havlik 1997). During 1993–97, the average labor intensity of the sample of the most competitive industries was still slightly higher, and the average capital intensity lower (except Slovenia—see table 13). Theoretical expectations regarding problems in capital-intensive industries, given the relative scarcity of capital on the one hand, and labor cost advantages of the CEECs on the other hand, are thus being confirmed. In addition other results partly confirm, but in some cases again differ from, the theoretical expectations. The sample of most competitive industries in the more developed CEECs (the Czech Republic, Hungary, and Slovenia) is characterized also by slightly higher than average R&D intensity; the energy intensity of the most competitive exports is rapidly declining, especially in the Czech Republic, Hungary, and Slovenia, (whereas it was still higher than average in Poland).

Another possible way of investigating the emerging export specialization patterns is to look at the relation of x-factor intensities and either the CEECs' recent performance in terms of export growth or the size of achieved market shares. One might expect that the largest market share gains

Table 13 X-Factor Intensities of Central and Eastern European Countries' Most Competitive Industries in Exports to the European Union(12), 1993–97

(Average x-factor intensity of top 50 competitive industries in percent of average for all 92 industries)

	Capital intensity	Labor intensity	R&D intensity	Skill intensity	Energy intensity
Czech Republic	87.84	101.25	125.42	100.24	86.27
Hungary	88.15	104.09	125.68	101.18	86.42
Poland	91.64	101.08	101.69	97.15	104.06
Slovenia	100.7	94.96	106.20	100.70	86.58

Note: The top 50 industries are those with largest absolute market share gains in the EU(12) during 1993–97. For factor intensities, see text.

Source: Own calculations based on Eurostat COMEXT database.

were recorded mainly by industries that use the relatively abundant factor more intensively (and vice versa). We find statistically significant (at 5 percent significance level, in a sample of 50 industries with the largest absolute market share gains), positive correlations between the 1993–97 export growth and x-factor intensity in the following cases (figure 10):[19]

- Capital intensity: Hungary;
- Labor intensity: Slovenia;
- R&D intensity: the Czech Republic and Hungary;
- Skill intensity: Hungary, and
- Energy intensity: Poland.

The positive correlation of export growth and capital intensity in Hungary could result from high FDI inflows, while in Slovenia, there is a highly significant negative correlation indicating the lack of capital. Contrary to expectations, there is a significant negative correlation between the labor intensity and recent export growth in Hungary (and in this case Slovenia shows a significant positive correlation), indicating that labor-intensive industries did not achieve high growth of exports in Hungary, but did in Slovenia. Both results are surprising, especially the case of Slovenia, as this is a country with relatively high labor costs. Another new feature is positive correlation of export growth with R&D-intensity in the Czech Republic and Hungary (in the latter country the export growth of skill-intensive industries is also evident). Hungary thus displays clear signs of positive export restructuring away from labor-intensive industries, and towards more capital-, R&D-, and skill-intensive manufacturing exports. A complementary exercise, useful for finding the current trade specialization patterns, is to correlate x-factor intensities of successful export industries with their achieved (in 1997) market shares in the EU(12). Here we find statistically significant (at a 5 percent level, again in the sample of 50 most competitive industries) positive correlation only for energy-intensive industries in Poland, as well as significant negative correlation of skill intensity and 1997 market shares in Poland and the Czech Republic (figure 11).

A surprise of this analysis is the lack of clear evidence for a growing specialization on labor-intensive industries (except Slovenia, which has much higher labor costs than other CEECs). No cor-

Figure 10 Correlation of X-Factor Intensities and Export Growth to the EU(12) for 50 Most Competitive Industries, 1993–97

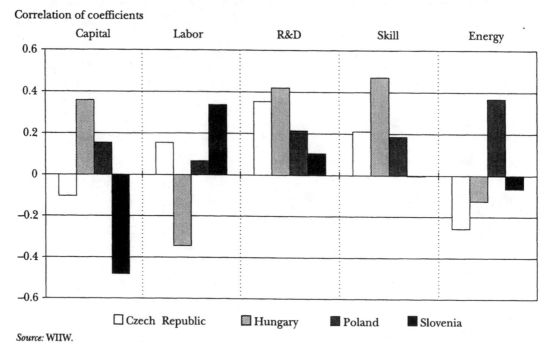

Source: WIIW.

Figure 11 Correlation of X-Factor Intensities and Market Shares in EU(12) for 50 Most Competitive Industries in 1997

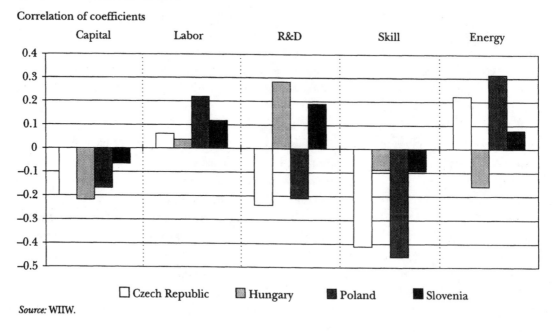

Source: WIIW.

relation could be detected between the achieved market shares of the most competitive industries and labor intensity in any of the CEECs. There is even a significantly negative correlation between the recent export growth and labor intensity in Hungary, possibly explained by the positive structural changes in the manufacturing industry, stimulated by the activity of foreign investors (Hunya 1998). There are apparently a few other countries (including less developed CEECs) which have taken place of low labor cost economies. Another explanation could be the fact that labor costs advantages are relatively small in the more developed CEECs. Another encouraging development is the good performance of R&D- and skill-intensive industries in Hungary (the former also in the Czech Republic). On the other hand, neither Poland nor Slovenia shows any straightforward pattern of trade restructuring.[20]

The Changing Pattern of the Central and Eastern European Countries' Revealed Comparative Advantage

Finally, we investigate industry-specific revealed comparative advantage (RCA) values in the CEECs' trade with the EU (12).[21] At first glance, the RCA pattern did not change much during the later phase of transition as compared with the beginning of the 1990s (Dobrinsky and Landesmann 1995). Even in the more recent period (after 1993), the biggest RCA values for CEECs have been observed in "traditional," less sophisticated industries such as cement, wood, textiles, clothing, footwear, and metals, whereas comparative disadvantages (negative RCA values) are located mainly in machinery, equipment, electrotechnical, and pharmaceuticals industries, as well as in a number of food industry sub-branches. In addition, from a dynamic perspective, there were just a few industries with improving (rising) RCA during 1993–97. A synthetic indicator, measuring the change of RCA in the 1996–97 period as compared with 1993–94, shows that about 80 percent of all CEECs' industries experienced declining RCA in the more recent period and the aggregate competitiveness of manufacturing industry worsened.[22] An improvement of RCA could be detected in a small number of industries (more in Poland, less in Hungary and Slovenia—see Annex D). But there is no apparent general pattern in RCA changes, either in the correlation among individual CEECs or in the correlation with different x-factor intensities.

More conclusive and interesting results reveal correlations between RCA values and x-factor intensities over the whole period from 1989 to 1997. Here the pattern is clear and the results are basically in line with the initial expectations: most CEECs display highly significant positive correlations between RCA values and labor- and energy-intensive industries, while having comparative disadvantages (negative correlations with RCA values) in skill-, R&D-, and capital-intensive industries (figure 12). But there were also some important changes in these trade specialization patterns during this period (for the Czech Republic and Slovenia, separate data are available only for the period 1993–97). Interesting developments can be discerned especially in the more recent period (after 1993):

- High, and mostly statistically significant, positive correlations of RCA values with labor-intensive industries. In Hungary, there seemed to be a move away from this specialization

Figure 12 Correlation of X-Factor Intensities with Revealed Comparative Advantage Values in Trade with the European Union(12), 1989–97

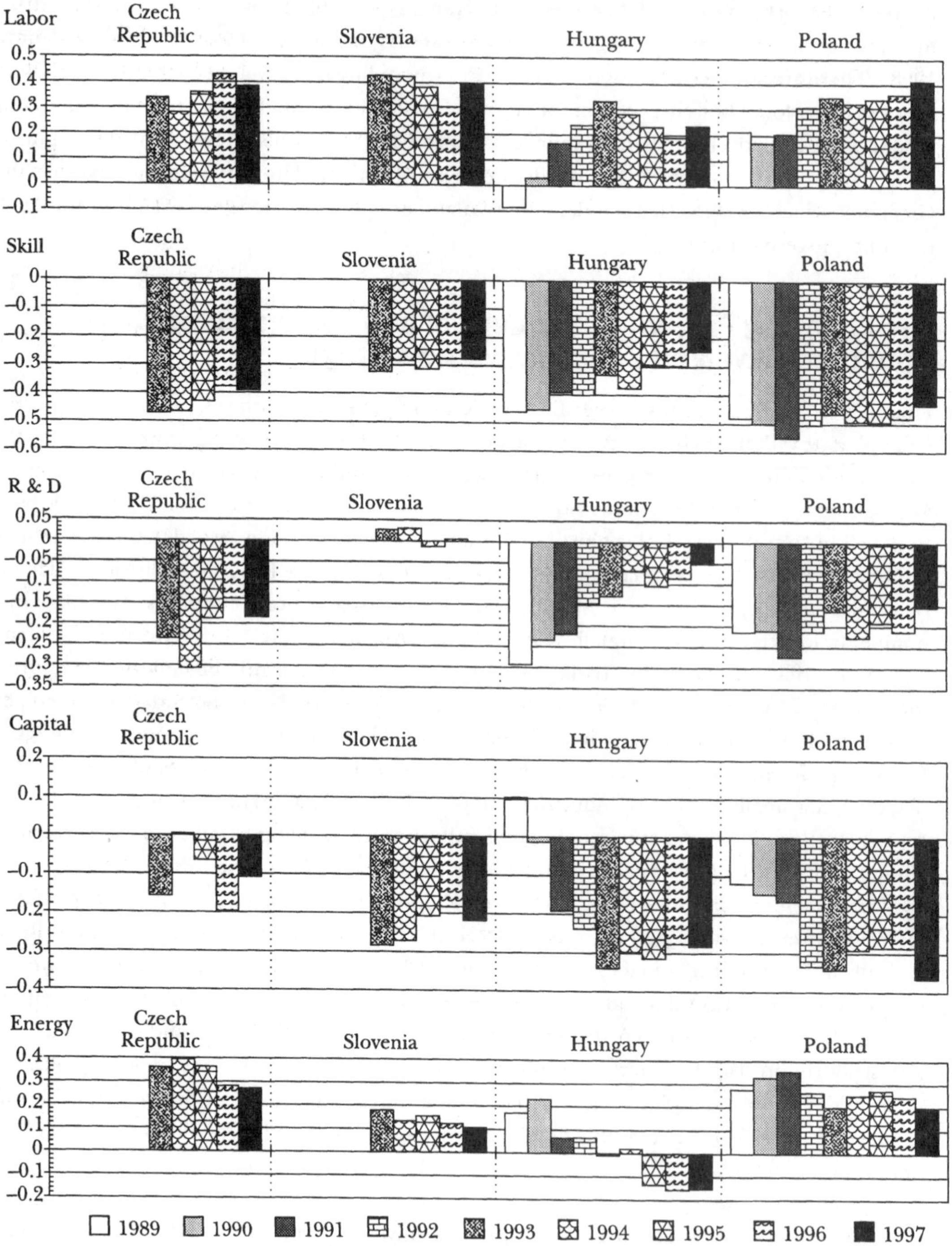

Source: WIIW.

pattern after 1993, while it continued in the Czech Republic and in Slovenia and increased in Poland. A persistence of this specialization pattern could lead to problems in view of high and growing ULCs in Slovenian and Polish manufacturing industries.

- Mostly negative (though statistically not significant) correlations between RCA values and R&D intensity. Moreover, the gap is clearly narrowing in Hungary and the Czech Republic, though less so in Poland.

- An even larger gap in skill-intensive industries (highly significant negative correlations with RCA values in most CEECs). There are again remarkable improvements in Hungary, Slovenia, and in the Czech Republic. In the two former countries the skill gap is not statistically significant anymore.

- Somewhat diminishing comparative disadvantages in capital-intensive industries after 1993 in Hungary (declining negative correlations of capital-intensity with RCA values) and persisting (and statistically significant) comparative disadvantages in Poland. This would suggest that the comparative lack of capital in Hungary is becoming less visible (an effect of FDI inflows).

- A markedly less pronounced specialization in energy-intensive sectors (declining positive correlations with RCA values) in the Czech Republic and Poland.

The above analysis thus largely confirms the theoretical expectations for the existing general comparative advantages of CEECs: relatively abundant (unskilled) labor, and still in some cases still energy, as opposed to the relative scarcity of capital, R&D, and skilled labor.[23] But there have been important changes during the recent (1993-97) period, with Hungary's trade restructuring advancing faster than in other CEECs (especially in closing the skill- and R&D gaps) while Poland and Slovenia's trade specialization patterns hardly changed for the better during the period 1989–97.

3. Foreign Direct Investment, Restructuring, and Competitiveness

Foreign and Domestic Sectors Compared

Foreign direct investment (FDI) is playing an increasingly important role in the CEECs. In the first years of transition, FDI was attracted by newly liberalized markets and by the sale offers of selected strategic companies.[24] By end-1998, about half of almost US$60 billion invested by foreign companies in the four CEECs was invested through privatization-related acquisitions.[25] Some 10–20 percent were green-field investments, the rest being investment into already existing foreign investment enterprises (FIEs). Mass privatization by vouchers, sales to insiders, or management buyouts have hindered foreign acquisitions, whereas in direct tenders foreigners usually outbid domestic investors. The main method of privatization has thus boosted FDI in Hungary, had no effect in Poland, and hindered FDI in the Czech Republic and Slovenia. As of end-1998, the stock of FDI reached $9.4 billion in the Czech Republic, $19 billion in Hungary, $28.5 billion in Poland, and $2.5 billion in Slovenia.[26]

Efficiency seeking investments were rare initially. With time, the market access has become less important and the costs factor started to prevail. The distribution of FDI by economic activities reflects the opening of individual sectors to foreign investment. Initially, most FDI went into trade and manufacturing; later it also went to the financial sector and telecommunications. In countries where new sectors were opened to foreign investment the share of manufacturing declined. The most notable examples were telecom privatizations in the Czech Republic and the gas and energy sectors in Hungary. The highest share of manufacturing investment has been registered in Poland where trade was privatized largely to domestic investors, and utilities have not yet been privatized. In Slovenia, where several activities are still closed to foreign investors and the manufacturing sector was privatized mainly to domestic owners, the energy sector has a remarkably high foreign share due to the atomic power station jointly owned with Croatia.

The foreign investment enterprises (companies with some share of foreign capital) are generally larger than domestic companies in terms of employment, and even more so in terms of nominal capital or assets per company (see Annex E).[27] The growing importance of FIEs was recorded in all CEECs by all indicators during 1994–97. This results partly from changes in company coverage, but an expansion of the foreign sector is quite apparent. The highest share of FIEs by all available indicators has been reached in Hungary where foreign penetration is on average 2 to 3 times higher than in Poland and the Czech Republic (table 14). Slovenia has generally lower penetration rates than the other three CEECs. The most dynamic increase of foreign penetration between 1994 and 1997 occurred in the Czech Republic and Poland. There has been a steady but relatively slow increase of foreign penetration in Hungary and Slovenia.

The high share of FIEs in employment and sales puts Hungary among the countries with the highest levels of foreign capital penetration in Europe. It seems that the foreign penetration in Hungarian manufacturing has already reached a level where further increases cannot be very dynamic. There is nevertheless still very intensive FDI activity in the form of capital increase in existing FIEs and the number of important green-field projects is growing. Sales and especially export sales were the indicators by which the share of FIEs increased fastest between 1994 and 1996. This indicates that the intensive foreign investment activity of the first half of the 1990s established competitive production capacities which expand more rapidly than in domestically owned companies. Foreign penetration in the Czech Republic almost doubled between 1994 and 1997 by most indicators. The foreign sector shows rapid expansion not only in terms of growing capital and sales, but also in terms of employment. Fifty thousand new manufacturing jobs were created in, or shifted to, the foreign sector, while the domestic sector lost 85 thousand jobs. Sales of products of FIEs increased by 130 percent, while the sales of domestic enterprises increased only by 14 percent (in current USD terms). Although ownership shifts cannot be followed with accuracy, it seems that the foreign sector was an important driving force of the recovery in the mid-1990s. The recent recession in the Czech Republic may have widened the gap between the crisis-ridden domestic and booming foreign sector, leading to a further increase in the share FIEs. In Poland, the penetration of foreign capital intensified only in the mid-1990s during an economic upswing. Poland's share of the foreign sector in manufacturing surpassed that of the Czech Republic in terms of all available indicators except employment and export shares. The latter indicates that FDI in Poland has been more domestic market–oriented. Slovenia has never had an FDI-friendly policy and the privatizations of the last few years did not allow foreign takeovers. Most of the large FIEs were already

Table 14 Foreign Investment Enterprises (FIEs) in Percent of All Manufacturing Industry Companies, 1997

	Equity capital	Employment	Investments	Sales/output	Export sales
Czech Republic[1]	—	16.0	31.2	26.3	42.0
Hungary	71.8[2]	42.8	79.8	66.7	75.4
Poland[3] (year 1996)	30.4	15	43.1	30.3	33.8
Slovenia (year 1996)	15.6	10.1	20.3	19.6	25.8

— Not available.
Note: 1. Companies with 25 and more employees. 2. Nominal capital in cash. 3. Corporate sector.
Source: Hunya (1999); Poland: Durka and others (1998); 1997 data for the Czech Republic: Zemplinerová (1998).

established several years earlier. Increasing shares of FIEs are thus due mostly to their better performance and a more dynamic growth in comparison to the domestic sector.

Survey data show that labor productivity in FIEs is on average up to two times higher than in domestic enterprises in all CEECs.[28] At the same time, FIEs pay, on the average, about 20–30 percent higher wages than domestic companies. This would imply that the overall labor cost advantages identified above are even more pronounced in FIEs operating in CEECs. The gap in performance between FIEs and domestic enterprises did not grow in the Czech Republic during 1994–96, whereas it decreased in Slovenia. In Hungary, the high and increasing productivity gap shows on one hand the FIEs' dynamism, and on the other hand it demonstrates an unhealthy duality between the foreign and domestic sectors. FIEs usually introduce improvements in technology, management, and marketing. The productivity advantage exists in both technical terms and in terms of higher product quality reflected in higher sales prices. If gaps (in technology, productivity, and so forth) between FIEs and the domestic sector are very large, the two segments of the economy may find it difficult to cooperate and the foreign sector functions as an enclave. In this case direct spillover effects are limited. At the same time, there is a learning process going on in domestic owned companies that may with time lead to narrower gaps between foreign and domestically owned companies.

The foreign investors use more recent, capital intensive and labor saving technology. The lead of FIEs in terms of capital intensity is especially pronounced in Hungary where capital-intensive industries (for example, the steel industry and oil refineries) are more open to foreign investors than in other CEECs. The relative capital intensity of FIEs, measured by the amount of nominal capital per employee, grew over time in Hungary and Slovenia and it declined in the Czech Republic. As to the difference in the amount of assets per employee, there has been an increase in the Czech Republic and a decline in Slovenia. The outstanding export performance relative to output indicates that FIEs are more export-oriented than domestic firms. This is confirmed by 1996 data for Hungary and Slovenia, and by 1997 data for the Czech Republic. Furthermore in the case of Poland the share of FIEs in exports is higher than their share in total sales. In Hungary, FIEs account for more than three-quarters of manufacturing exports, and the difference between export intensity of the domestic and the foreign sector has been growing. A high degree of export-orientation is coupled with high import intensity as well. FIEs in Hungary and Poland, for which data are available, show a clearly negative foreign trade balance.

FIEs invest more than domestic companies and have thus a positive effect on economic growth and restructuring. Investment data also suggest that foreign investors rapidly restructure acquired manufacturing firms. Production restructuring is usually connected with layoffs. Foreign penetration may thus increase unemployment in the short run, but also generate more new jobs later. Investments of FIEs are mostly financed by retained profits, which thus may not be repatriated on a massive scale. Although the current account data sometime show increasing profit repatriation, the FIEs' reinvestment of profits is also growing. As long as CEECs remain favorable locations for FDI in terms of expected profit, there is no reason why most profits should be repatriated.[29] The effects of FDI are thus far from unequivocal; a number of negative aspects can emerge as well. Short-term problems may also appear due to fast restructuring, resulting in capacity destruction and layoffs. These problems may generate not only social and regional inequalities, but growing foreign trade deficits as well.

The presence of foreign capital in CEEC manufacturing industries is very uneven. The first three most important branches made up about half of the capital controlled by foreign investors in 1996 (67.3 percent for the Czech Republic, 47.7 percent for Hungary, 53.3 percent for Slovenia, and 55.3 percent for Poland—see Annex E), though the concentration is declining. The main branch with above-average foreign penetration is manufacturing of transport equipment (DM), most notably motor vehicles. This is the industry where FIE shares in capital and sales are usually the highest in CEECs. The second branch generally dominated by the sales of FIEs is manufacturing of electrical machinery and equipment (DL). Next comes the food industry (DA), which has about average foreign penetration rates in all CEECs. High shares of FIEs thus appear in both domestic-oriented branches like food, beverages, and tobacco, and in predominantly export-oriented industries like motor vehicles and electrical machinery.

Conclusions and Policy Recommendations

All CEECs are competitive due to their low labor costs. Even Slovenian nominal wages—about three times higher than in other CEECs—are much lower than in the EU. The assessment of wage developments varies widely depending on the comparison made. Wages in foreign currency have been growing faster than domestic wages, and product wages grew faster than consumer wages. Such differences may lead not only to widely different analytic and policy conclusions, but potentially to conflicting reactions by foreign investors, domestic producers, and wage earners (trade unions). Aggregate productivity grew faster than product wages during the 1990s in Hungary and in Slovenia and wage competitiveness thus improved. In Poland and the Czech Republic, productivity growth lagged considerably behind increases in product wages and competitiveness thus deteriorated. Whereas in the Czech Republic excessive wage growth was at least halted in 1998, policy corrections aimed at restoring wage competitiveness might soon become necessary in Poland. Manufacturing industry wages are not much different from averages for the whole economy. But there are growing wage differences across individual manufacturing industry branches. Compared with average wage growth, wages have been generally declining in the textiles and leather industries while, on the other hand, rapidly growing relative wages are observed in the paper and printing industry and in the coke and refined petroleum industry, as well as in chemicals. In most CEECs, relative wages increased also in the foreign-dominated transport equipment industry.

CEECs productivity and quality gaps partly eliminate their cost advantages arising from the low wages. The analysis of unit labor costs developments at the macro level shows that the labor cost competitiveness has deteriorated since the early 1990s in the Czech Republic, Poland, and Slovenia, while it has markedly improved with declining ULCs in Hungary. This can also be attributed—apart from other factors (including slow overall wage growth)—to much higher foreign investment penetration in this country. In particular, a more intensive involvement of foreign investors in the Hungarian manufacturing industry has brought about large efficiency gains. Hungarian labor cost competitiveness in manufacturing industry markedly improved recently, and in several branches ULCs have dropped below the level of the Czech Republic and Poland. The growth of Slovenian manufacturing industry ULCs has been modest, but their level is still about twice as high as in the remaining three CEECs. Wage growth and currency appreciation that is not accompanied by corresponding productivity improvements leads to a deterioration of costs competitiveness. This deterioration may cause external disequilibrium that then requires painful policy adjustments. Such problems occurred in Hungary in 1995 and in the Czech Republic in 1997. Recent developments indicate that Poland could become vulnerable soon as well. On the other hand, Slovenia stands out as a permanently high-wage country among other CEECs, so far apparently without encountering any serious worsening of competitiveness.

The relative unit labor costs (compared to Austria) in more sophisticated branches of industry like transport, electrical, and optical equipment are even lower in the CEECs than average for manufacturing industry. In enterprises with foreign ownership, where management practices, quality control standards, and marketing channels help to substantially raise the average productivity (while still maintaining considerable wage gaps), the labor cost advantages are even more pronounced. Foreign investment enterprises clearly outperform domestic firms on most accounts. Still, the recent Hungarian experience shows that high FDI cannot be solely relied upon and measures aimed at the promotion of domestic sector's development are equally important.

The analysis of emerging export specialization patterns has shown that the foreign penetrated industries are highly competitive in exports to the EU. Furthermore labor productivity gaps between foreign and domestically owned enterprises are evident at the level of individual industrial branches as well. Low productivity (growth) usually occurs in industries and countries with lower than average foreign penetration. On the other hand, the highest productivity improvements can be associated with above average foreign penetration in a branch. Figures 13 and 14 illustrate how high foreign penetration of manufacturing industry has been associated with huge ULC improvements in Hungary, whereas a lower foreign penetration coincided with deteriorating labor cost competitiveness in the Czech Republic (at least until 1996). But even here we find branches with higher than average foreign penetration and impressive ULC improvements (for example, DL—transport equipment).

The evidence for emerging trade specialization and competitiveness patterns is still mixed. Trade liberalizations entailed in the EU-CEEC Association Agreements have led to a significant trade expansion. But despite low labor costs, asymmetric trade liberalizations in favor of CEECs, and CEECs' substantial market share gains in the EU, the growing trade surpluses of the EU suggest that exporters from the EU have in fact been much more competitive. Trade restructuring has proceeded at a fast pace. In the more recent period (since 1993), a number of sophisticated branches of CEECs' manufacturing industry became competitive as well. Nevertheless, CEECs' revealed comparative advantages are still mostly in labor-intensive industries. But the Hungarian move away from this specialization pattern (and also some closure of skill and R&D gaps) illustrates positive effects of foreign investments on restructuring. On the other hand, a slower pace of trade restructuring identified in the Czech Republic and Slovenia (and some deterioration in Poland) could lead to problems in integration and competition with the EU.

Figure 13 Czech Republic: Unit Labor Cost Growth (ECU) and Foreign Penetration

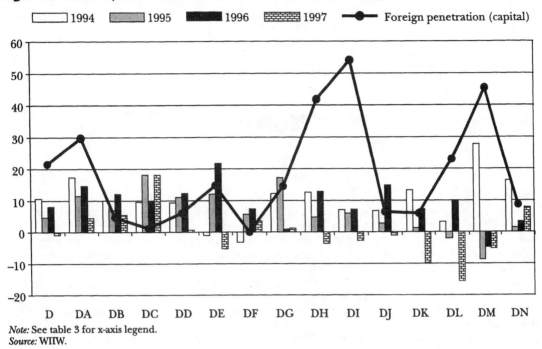

Note: See table 3 for x-axis legend.
Source: WIIW.

Figure 14 Hungary: Unit Labor Cost (ECU) and Foreign Penetration

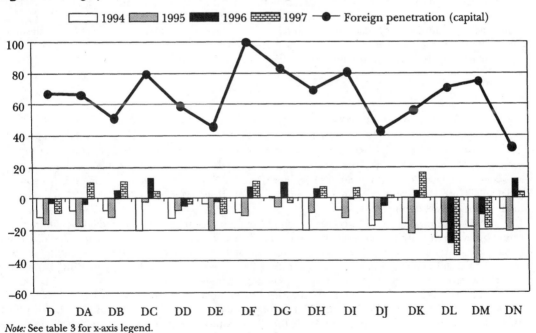

Note: See table 3 for x-axis legend.
Source: WIIW.

Notes

1. According to the latest Eurostat estimates, Slovenia's real per capita GDP amounted to 68 percent of the fifteen EU countries' average in 1997, that of the Czech Republic to 63 percent, of Hungary to 47 percent and of Poland to 40 percent. Slovenia's per capita GDP level is thus only slightly lower than that of either Greece or Portugal (see Eurostat 1998). Reflecting the progress in institutional reforms, the Czech Republic, Hungary, and Poland are already members of the Organization for Economic Cooperation and Development (OECD); Slovenia's OECD membership will follow soon.

2. Benchmark purchasing power parity (PPP) estimates were adopted from OECD (1998). We have converted the original benchmark purchasing power parity standards for the year 1996 calculated for 28 OECD countries to European Currency units (ECU), and extrapolated with GDP price deflators (for details of the estimation method see Havlik, 1996).

3. The equilibrium wages were estimated from a cross-country regression by Krajnyak and Zettelmayer (1997) and updated by the EBRD. See EBRD (1998), p. 66. Slovenia is not included in the sample.

4. Price/quality gaps are one of the reasons why most CEEC export products are located in lower price/quality segments, though the existing gaps could already have been reduced at the time of writing, especially in Hungary, Poland, and Slovenia (less so in the Czech Republic)—see Landesmann and Burgstaller (1997 and 1999). The existence of quality gaps is also documented by studies indicating that the physical productivity in manufacturing plants is substantially higher than the productivity estimated from the value added (see Hitchens and others (1995).

5. Unit labor costs (ULCs) are defined as:

$$ULC_t = W_t / Prod_t$$

where W_t is the average annual gross wage (computed as 12 times average monthly gross wage) and $Prod_t$ is GDP per employed person at 1996 prices. In order to estimate changes of ULCs in international currency (we use here ECU), the $ULCs_t$ were adjusted for exchange rate changes by dividing national ULCs by the nominal ECU exchange rate. The level comparison of ULCs presented below is obtained from the exchange rate–adjusted ULCs after multiplication by the benchmark PPP for 1996. Such adjustment is necessary in order to get a rough approximation of comparative productivity levels in the base year (for more on the methodology see Oulton 1994).

6. The level comparison of ULCs can be obtained from the exchange rate–adjusted ULCs after multiplication by the benchmark PPP for 1996. For recent productivity estimates in the OECD area and discussion of other methodological issues, see Pilat (1996). Unfortunately, Pilat explicitly excludes the new OECD members (The Czech Republic, Hungary and Poland); see Pilat (1996), p. 3. In addition, the EBRD's *Transition Report 1998* provides a table only analysis with percentage changes of ULCs in industry (see EBRD 1998).

7. Austria served as a bridge for earlier East-West PPP comparisons in the framework of the European Comparison Project (ECP). More recent PPP data for the year 1996 was compiled by the OECD (see OECD 1998). Comparable wage data are not available for all EU countries either. Again, note that the exchange

rate–based productivity and ULC comparison is not the proper indicator and is shown in table 4 only for illustration (see Pilat 1996).

8. Indirect wage costs are about 30-40 percent of total labor costs (about 24 percent in Slovenia), also lower than in the majority of the EU countries (see table 1 and Annex B). Austrian total labor costs (in the manufacturing industry in 1997) were ATS271.5 per hour (ECU19.6), among the highest in the OECD area (see Wirtschaftskammer Österreich 1998).

9. Industrial productivity is estimated from real gross industrial production per employee; ULC changes are computed from changes in nominal gross wages (in ECU terms) relative to changes in labor productivity. In addition, the sample of enterprises covered varies not only by country but in individual years as well (see table 1).

10. In Austria and the majority of other EU countries, the differences between both price levels were much less pronounced (in 1996 about 2 percent in Austria, representing 1 percent of the EU average). Relative prices of machinery and equipment in CEECs were close to the OECD average and therefore higher than the overall price level in the CEECs (see OECD 1998, Dietz, 1999).

11. PPP for gross fixed capital formation—PPPCAP—is a probable upper boundary for CEECs' comparable price levels and thus the lower boundary for productivity comparisons. Alternative approaches, using, for example, "unit value ratios" for similar products as purchasing power parities or other adjustments, could not be used because of the lack of data for the transition countries (see van Ark 1992). For the merits and drawbacks of different approaches see also Pilat (1996).

12. The relatively small productivity lead of Slovenia is indirectly confirmed by "price gap" measures in exports to the EU (see Landesmann and Burgstaller 1999).

13. See the standard deviations in tables 3 and 6. Labor productivity in the manufacturing industry is again estimated from gross output per employee. Part of the difference in labor productivity has to be attributed to different capital productivity, especially in capital-intensive branches. Differences in total productivity would probably be lower.

14. Data on the structure of total labor costs are shown in Annex B. For Slovenia we assumed a flat rate for indirect wage costs at 24 percent of total labor costs in all branches of manufacturing. For Austria, where labor costs in a detailed NACE classification are not available, we used data published by Wirtschaftskammer Österreich (1998). Austrian direct labor costs include bonuses, especially the obligatory 13th and 14th salaries, which are here de facto a part of direct wage costs.

15. We use EU(12) in order to ensure comparability with the period prior to 1995 EU enlargement.

16. This is another reason why existing trade theories have so far not been very conclusive in explaining the trade patterns of the CEECs. An earlier study, covering trade specialization of Czechoslovakia, Hungary and Poland in the period of "passive restructuring" during 1989–92, revealed in part different specialization patterns (see Havlik 1995).

17. "Competitive gain" is here defined as the gain of market shares in the EU(12), weighted by the value of exports of a particular industry in the base year (1993). A negative "structural effect" (registered especially in Poland and Slovenia) means that CEECs specialize in export products for which demand is growing at below average in the EU; the effect of "general demand" measures the growth of total extra-EU imports (see Havlik 1995).

18. Lacking other data, we used at this stage of research factor intensities derived for the four largest EU countries (Germany, France, Italy, and the United Kingdom) (see Landesmann 1995 and *European Economy* (1995). This is one of the drawbacks of our methods, since the factor intensities of CEEC industries will most likely differ. Following other authors using these EU factor intensities we assume that at least the ranking of industries by the different factor intensities correlates across CEECs and EU countries. The EU factor intensities, available for 92 NACE industries, were approximated by the following indicators:

- Labor intensity: Number of employees/Output
- Skill intensity: Non-manual labor/Total employment
- R&D intensity: R&D expenditure/Output
- Capital intensity: Cumulative investment/Number of employees
- Energy intensity: Energy costs/Output.

19. Correlation coefficients greater than 0.3 are statistically significant at the 5 percent level.

20. These broadly similar results which indicate a shift towards higher value-added exports between 1993 and 1996 in Hungary and in the Czech Republic, and little if any change in Poland and Slovenia, were also obtained by the UN ECE (1998).

21. RCA (revealed comparative advantage) value compares the ratio of exports and imports in a particular industry with the ratio of total exports to imports:

$$\mathrm{RCA}_{it} = \ln \left[\left(E_{it} / I_{it} \right) / \left(E_{tot} / I_{tot} \right) \right] * 100$$

A higher RCA$_i$ in year t reveals a comparative advantage of industry i (see Balassa 1965). In this case we take into account all 92 industries for which x-factor intensities are available.

22. This reflects growing deficits in the CEECs' overall manufacturing industry trade. RCA improvement (deterioration) is here evaluated with the help of the average growth (decline) of RCA for 1996 and 1997 as compared with the average for 1993 and 1994, in order to eliminate annual fluctuations. Negative RCA values of food industry sub-branches can in part be attributed to still-existing restrictions in agro-food trade, though there was some improvement recently.

23. Again, broadly similar results were obtained by the UN ECE secretariat using different data set and methodology (see UN ECE 1998).

24. This section draws heavily on Hunya (1998, 1999).

25. All dollar amounts in this paper are U.S. unless otherwise indicated.

26. See Hunya and Stankovsky (1998).

27. Performance indicators of the foreign investment sector were derived from company income statements. The analysis is based on a Phare-ACE project that set up a joint framework for studying the manner and impact of FDI penetration on CEECs. The Database on Foreign Investment Enterprises in Central European Countries was published by the WIIW in September 1998. Data refer to 1996, and the database is biased towards large companies. While in Hungary, Poland, and Slovenia only very small ventures fall out, while most of the data for the Czech Republic cover only companies with 100 or more employees.

28. The comparison of FIE penetration rates by production and employment in OECD countries' manufacturing also indicates that the productivity of FIEs is higher. The lead of FIEs in terms of labor productivity is thus not specific to CEECs, though the size of the productivity gap is especially large in their case. In OECD countries, the productivity advantage of FIEs compared to the average productivity of the manufacturing industry is 30 percent, and in the CEECs about 70–90 percent (see Hunya 1999).

29. However, the latest deterioration of the Hungarian current account (largely attributable to a higher profit repatriation by FIE) raises new policy dilemmas (see Hunya and Richter 1999).

Annex A

Table A.1 Prices, Exchange Rates, and Unit Labor Costs (ULC), 1990-98
(ECU-based annual averages)

	1990	1992	1993	1994	1995	1996	1997	1998 prelim.
Czech Republic								
Producer price index, 1989=100	104.3	195.3	213.3	224.5	241.6	253.0	265.4	278.4
Consumer price index, 1989=100	109.7	190.8	230.5	253.5	276.7	301.0	326.6	361.6
GDP deflator, 1989=100	109.2	186.5	219.8	243.6	267.5	293.2	312.3	346.6
Exchange rate (ER), CZK/ECU	22.89	36.62	34.10	34.06	34.31	34.01	35.80	36.16
ER nominal, 1989=100	137.9	220.6	205.4	205.2	206.7	204.9	215.7	217.9
Real ER (CPI-based), 1989=100	131.3	132.3	103.2	95.8	91.7	85.2	84.1	77.5
Real ER (PPI-based), 1989=100	138.1	129.2	111.6	108.2	105.0	101.4	103.5	100.6
PPP, CZK/ECU	5.65	8.82	10.27	11.13	11.79	12.68	13.26	14.57
ERDI (ECU based)	4.05	4.15	3.32	3.06	2.91	2.68	2.70	2.48
Average monthly gross wages, CZK	3286	4644	5817	6894	8172	9676	10696	11688
Average monthly gross wages, ECU (ER)	144	127	171	202	238	285	299	323
Average monthly gross wages, ECU (PPP)	581	527	566	619	693	763	807	802
GDP nominal, bn CZK	579.3	846.8	1004.1	1148.7	1381.1	1572.3	1680.0	1820.7
Employment total, 1000 persons	5351.2	4927.1	4848.3	4884.8	5011.6	5044.4	4993.3	4871.0
GDP per employed person, CZK	108255	171874	207098	235153	275578	311691	336452	373784
GDP per empl. person, CZK at 1996 pr.	290744	270217	276269	282964	302072	311691	315852	316187
Unit labour costs, 1989=100	101.5	154.3	189.0	218.7	242.9	278.7	304.0	331.9
Unit labour costs, ER adj., 1989=100	73.6	69.9	92.0	106.6	117.5	136.0	141.0	152.3
Unit labour costs, PPP adj., Austria=100	17.85	15.01	18.32	20.84	21.82	25.92	28.34	30.84
Hungary								
Producer price index, 1989=100	122.0	180.3	199.8	222.4	286.7	349.2	420.4	467.9
Consumer price index, 1989=100	128.9	214.0	262.1	311.4	399.3	493.5	583.8	667.3
GDP deflator, 1989=100	125.7	191.6	232.5	277.9	348.8	422.7	500.7	567.8
Exchange rate (ER), HUF/ECU	80.48	102.10	107.50	124.78	162.65	191.15	210.93	240.98
ER, nominal 1989=100	123.7	156.9	165.2	191.8	250.0	293.8	324.2	370.3
Real ER (CPI-based), 1989=100	100.3	83.9	73.0	72.9	76.8	74.5	70.7	71.4
Real ER (PPI-based), 1989=100	105.9	99.6	95.7	102.1	107.0	105.3	98.2	101.8
PPP, HUF/ECU	28.02	39.00	46.76	54.64	66.19	78.67	91.51	102.75
ERDI (ECU based)	2.87	2.62	2.30	2.28	2.46	2.43	2.30	2.35
Average monthly gross wages, HUF	13446	22294	27173	33309	38900	46837	57270	67764
Average monthly gross wages, ECU (ER)	167	218	253	267	239	245	272	281
Average monthly gross wages, ECU (PPP)	480	572	581	610	588	595	626	660
GDP nominal, bn HUF	2089.3	2942.7	3548.3	4364.8	5614.0	6893.9	8540.7	10180.2
Employment total, 1000 persons	5385.8	4082.7	3827.3	3751.5	3678.8	3648.1	3646.3	3697.7
GDP per employed person, HUF	387928	720773	927103	1163481	1526041	1889723	2342292	2753117
GDP per empl. person, HUF at 1996 pr.	1304540	1590124	1685732	1769797	1849582	1889723	1977436	2049590
Unit labour costs, 1989=100	129.4	176.0	202.3	236.2	264.0	311.1	363.5	415.0
Unit labour costs, ER adj., 1989=100	104.6	112.2	122.5	123.2	105.6	105.9	112.1	112.1
Unit labour costs, PPP adj., Austria=100	28.73	27.27	27.61	27.27	22.21	22.85	25.53	25.69

(table continued on next page)

39

Table A.1 continued

	1990	1992	1993	1994	1995	1996	1997	1998 prelim.
Poland								
Producer price index, 1989=100	722.4	1368.9	1806.0	2262.6	2837.2	3189.0	3578.0	3839.6
Consumer price index, 1989=100	685.8	1670.1	2259.9	2987.6	3818.1	4577.9	5260.0	5880.7
GDP deflator, 1989=100	580.1	1247.8	1628.9	2091.3	2674.6	3174.9	3620.0	4055.5
Exchange rate (ER), PLN/ECU	1.209	1.768	2.119	2.696	3.135	3.377	3.706	3.923
ER, nominal, 1989=100	758.5	1108.7	1329.1	1690.7	1966.1	2118.3	2324.1	2460.5
Real ER (CPI-based), 1989=100	115.6	75.9	68.1	67.0	63.2	57.9	56.3	53.8
Real ER (PPI-based), 1989=100	109.7	92.7	85.2	88.5	85.0	83.2	82.8	82.4
PPP, PLN/ECU	0.3238	0.6361	0.8205	1.0297	1.2711	1.4797	1.6569	1.8379
ERDI (ECU based)	3.73	2.78	2.58	2.62	2.47	2.28	2.24	2.13
Average monthly gross wages, PLN	103	290	390	525	691	874	1066	1239
Average monthly gross wages, ECU (ER)	85	164	184	195	220	259	288	316
Average monthly gross wages, ECU (PPP)	318	456	476	510	544	591	643	674
GDP nominal, bn PLN	56.0	114.9	155.8	210.4	306.3	385.4	469.4	551.1
Employment total, 1000 persons	16280.0	14676.6	14330.1	14474.5	14735.2	15020.6	15438.7	15491.3
GDP per employed person, PLN	3441	7832	10871	14536	20788	25661	30402	35575
GDP per empl. person, PLN at 1996 pr.	18835	19927	21188	22069	24677	25661	26664	27851
Unit labour costs, 1989=100	584.0	1553.4	1968.7	2541.8	2991.4	3640.1	4270.4	4754.8
Unit labour costs, ER adj., 1989=100	77.0	140.1	148.1	150.3	152.2	171.8	183.7	193.2
Unit labour costs, PPP adj., Austria=100	19.07	30.72	30.11	30.02	28.85	33.44	37.73	39.95
Trade balance, ECU mn	3765.9	-2277.7	-3898.4	-3645.3	-4781.1	-10188.9	-14685.8	-16393.9
Producer price index, 1989=100	490.4	3469.6	4218.9	4965.8	5601.3	5982.4	6347.2	6728.1
Consumer price index, 1989=100	651.6	4305.1	5721.7	6923.3	7857.9	8635.7	9360.9	10100.5
GDP deflator, 1989=100	590.8	3549.2	4865.6	5964.4	6869.2	7634.4	8304.0	8912.5
Exchange rate (ER), SIT/ECU	14.39	105.02	132.28	152.36	153.12	169.51	180.40	186.27
ER, nominal, 1989=100	446.0	3254.8	4099.7	4722.1	4745.5	5253.6	5591.0	5772.9
Real ER (CPI-based), 1989=100	71.5	86.5	83.0	80.8	74.1	76.2	76.1	73.5
Real ER (PPI-based), 1989=100	95.0	107.3	112.5	112.6	104.0	109.9	112.2	110.3
PPP, SIT/ECU	9.76	53.52	72.50	86.88	96.58	105.26	112.44	119.49
ERDI (ECU based)	1.47	1.96	1.82	1.75	1.59	1.61	1.60	1.56
Average monthly gross wages, SIT	10172	51044	75432	94618	111996	129125	144251	158069
Average monthly gross wages, ECU (ER)	707	486	570	621	731	762	800	849
Average monthly gross wages, ECU (PPP)	1042	954	1040	1089	1160	1227	1283	1323
GDP nominal, bn SIT	196.8	1018.0	1435.1	1853.0	2221.5	2555.4	2907.3	3243.5
Employment total, 1000 persons	909.7	784.1	755.9	746.2	745.2	741.7	743.4	745.2
GDP per employed person, SIT	216283	1298330	1898598	2483125	2980876	3445175	3910621	4352685
GDP per empl. person, SIT at 1996 pr.	2794637	2792739	2979012	3178364	3312933	3445175	3595258	3728457
Unit labour costs, 1989=100	483.8	2429.4	3365.6	3956.9	4493.4	4981.8	5333.0	5635.1
Unit labour costs, ER adj., 1989=100	108.5	74.6	82.1	83.8	94.7	94.8	95.4	97.6
Unit labour costs, PPP adj., Austria=100	75.92	46.24	47.16	47.27	50.74	52.13	55.33	57.01

Note:

ER = Exchange Rate, PPP = Purchasing Power Parity, ERDI = Exchange Rate Deviation Index (all in terms of national currency per ECU). Benchmark PPPs for 1996 were estimated from purchasing parity standards for OECD (28) average and extrapolated with GDP price deflators.

Sources: BENCHMARK RESULTS OF THE 1996 EUROSTAT-OECD COMPARISON BY ANALYTICAL CATEGORIES, OECD, 1999; National statistics; WIFO; WIIW estimates.

Table A.2 Wages, Productivity, and Unit Labor Costs (ULC), 1990–98
(Annual changes in percent)

	1990	1992	1993	1994	1995	1996	1997	1998 prelim.
Czech Republic								
Exchange rate (ER), CZK/ECU	37.9	0.1	-6.9	-0.1	0.7	-0.9	5.3	1.0
Real ER (CPI-based)	31.3	-5.2	-22.0	-7.2	-4.3	-7.0	-1.3	-7.9
Real ER (PPI-based)	38.1	-4.2	-13.7	-3.0	-3.0	-3.4	2.1	-2.8
Average gross wages, CZK	3.7	22.5	25.3	18.5	18.5	18.4	10.5	9.3
Average gross wages, real (PPI based)	-0.6	11.4	14.7	12.6	10.2	13.1	5.4	4.2
Average gross wages, real (CPI based)	-5.5	10.2	3.7	7.8	8.6	8.8	1.9	-1.3
Average gross wages, ECU (ER)	-24.8	22.4	34.5	18.7	17.7	19.4	5.0	8.2
Employment total	-1.0	-2.6	-1.6	-0.8	2.6	0.7	-1.0	-2.4
GDP per empl. person, CZK at 1996 pr.	2.2	-0.7	2.2	2.4	6.8	3.2	1.3	0.1
Unit labour costs, CZK at 1996 prices	1.5	23.4	22.5	15.7	11.0	14.8	9.1	9.2
Unit labour costs, ER (ECU) adjusted	-26.4	23.3	31.6	15.8	10.2	15.8	3.6	8.1
Hungary								
Exchange rate (ER), HUF/ECU	23.7	10.1	5.3	16.1	30.3	17.5	10.3	14.2
Real ER (CPI-based)	0.3	-5.8	-13.0	-0.1	5.4	-3.0	-5.1	0.9
Real ER (PPI-based)	5.9	4.0	-3.8	6.6	4.8	-1.5	-6.7	3.6
Average gross wages, HUF	27.2	24.3	21.9	22.6	16.8	20.4	22.3	18.3
Average gross wages, real (PPI based)	4.3	11.5	10.0	10.1	-9.4	-1.1	1.6	6.3
Average gross wages, real (CPI based)	-1.3	1.1	-0.5	3.2	-8.9	-2.6	3.4	3.5
Average gross wages, ECU (ER)	2.8	12.9	15.8	5.6	-10.4	2.5	10.8	3.6
Employment total	-1.9	-19.1	-6.3	-2.0	-1.9	-0.8	0.0	1.4
GDP per empl. person, HUF at 1996 pr.	-1.7	19.8	6.0	5.0	4.5	2.2	4.6	3.6
Unit labour costs, HUF at 1996 prices	29.4	3.8	15.0	16.8	11.7	17.8	16.9	14.2
Unit labour costs, ER (ECU) adjusted	4.6	-5.8	9.2	0.6	-14.3	0.3	5.9	-0.1
Poland								
Exchange rate (ER), PLN/ECU	658.5	34.7	19.9	27.2	16.3	7.7	9.7	5.9
Real ER (CPI-based)	15.6	-0.9	-10.3	-1.6	-5.7	-8.3	-2.8	-4.4
Real ER (PPI-based)	9.7	5.4	-8.0	3.8	-3.9	-2.2	-0.5	-0.4
Average gross wages, PLN	397.9	65.0	34.8	34.5	31.6	26.5	21.9	16.3
Average gross wages, real (PPI based)	-31.1	22.7	2.1	7.3	4.9	12.6	8.6	8.4
Average gross wages, real (CPI based)	-27.4	15.4	-0.4	1.7	3.0	5.5	6.1	4.0
Average gross wages, ECU (ER)	-34.4	22.5	12.4	5.7	13.2	17.4	11.1	9.8
Employment total	-4.2	-4.2	-2.4	1.0	1.8	1.9	2.8	0.3
GDP per empl. person, PLN at 1996 pr.	-14.8	7.1	6.3	4.2	11.8	4.0	3.9	4.5
Unit labour costs, PLN at 1996 prices	484.0	54.0	26.7	29.1	17.7	21.7	17.3	11.3
Unit labour costs, ER (ECU) adjusted	-23.0	14.3	5.7	1.5	1.2	12.9	6.9	5.2
Slovak Republic								
Exchange rate (ER), SKK/ECU	38.5	0.4	-1.8	5.4	1.4	-0.1	-1.2	4.3
Real ER (CPI-based)	31.1	-3.9	-19.3	-5.0	-4.4	-3.6	-5.2	-1.4
Real ER (PPI-based)	38.1	0.4	-15.2	-2.3	-3.6	-2.2	-3.8	1.9
Average gross wages, SKK	4.1	20.5	18.4	17.0	14.3	13.3	13.1	8.4
Average gross wages, real (PPI based)	-0.7	14.4	1.0	6.1	4.9	8.8	8.3	5.0
Average gross wages, real (CPI based)	-5.7	9.5	-3.9	3.2	4.0	7.1	6.6	1.6
Average gross wages, ECU (ER)	-24.8	20.0	20.6	11.0	12.8	13.5	14.5	4.0
Employment total	-0.8	-11.7	-0.1	-1.8	2.2	0.8	0.2	-0.4
GDP per empl. person, SKK at 1996 pr.	-1.6	5.8	-3.7	6.7	4.7	5.7	6.3	4.9
Unit labour costs, SKK at 1996 prices	5.9	13.8	22.9	9.6	9.2	7.2	6.4	3.4
Unit labour costs, ER (ECU) adjusted	-23.5	13.4	25.2	4.0	7.7	7.3	7.7	-0.9

(table continued on next page)

Table A.2 continued

	1990	1992	1993	1994	1995	1996	1997	1998 prelim.
Slovenia								
Exchange rate (ER), SIT/ECU	346.0	208.7	26.0	15.2	0.5	10.7	6.4	3.3
Real ER (CPI-based)	-28.5	5.7	-4.1	-2.7	-8.2	2.8	-0.1	-3.4
Real ER (PPI-based)	-5.0	2.9	4.9	0.1	-7.7	5.8	2.1	-1.7
Average gross wages, SIT	379.6	203.4	47.8	25.4	18.4	15.3	11.7	9.6
Average gross wages, real (PPI based)	-2.2	-3.9	21.5	6.6	4.9	8.0	5.3	3.4
Average gross wages, real (CPI based)	-26.4	-1.3	11.2	3.7	4.3	4.9	3.1	1.6
Average gross wages, ECU (ER)	7.5	-1.7	17.3	8.9	17.8	4.1	5.0	6.1
Employment total	-3.9	-6.5	-3.6	-1.3	-0.1	-0.5	0.2	0.2
GDP per empl. person, SIT at 1996 pr.	-0.9	1.2	6.7	6.7	4.2	4.0	4.4	3.7
Unit labour costs, SIT at 1996 prices	383.8	200.0	38.5	17.6	13.6	10.9	7.1	5.7
Unit labour costs, ER (ECU) adjusted	8.5	-2.8	10.0	2.1	13.0	0.1	0.6	2.3

Sources: National statistics and WIIW estimates.

42

Annex B

Table B.1.1 Czech Republic—Production Growth
(Annual changes in percent)

		1990	1991	1992	1993	1994	1995	1996	1997	1993-97
D	Manufacturing total	-5.1	-26.3	-7.9	-8.2	-0.2	8.2	4.6	7.1	2.1
DA	Food products; beverages and tobacco	-3.4	1.8	-11.1	-5.1	-1.8	4.2	4.4	4.2	1.1
DB	Textiles and textile products	-2.1	-31.8	-6.2	-14.8	-2.3	0.7	-5.4	-2.0	-4.9
DC	Leather and leather products	-1.8	-27.9	-25.4	-2.2	-3.2	-10.4	-6.2	-24.8	-9.8
DD	Wood and wood products	-14.0	-16.2	-14.2	-17.2	1.0	2.8	-2.4	4.9	-2.5
DE	Pulp, paper & paper products; publishing & printing	-5.3	-13.6	14.3	-8.3	19.0	1.8	-4.6	12.2	3.5
DF	Coke, refined petroleum products & nuclear fuel	-11.8	-35.5	-11.0	-8.1	8.0	7.1	6.5	-0.1	2.5
DG	Chemicals, chemical products and man-made fibres	-6.5	-28.5	49.5	-7.4	2.5	-1.0	11.6	0.9	1.1
DH	Rubber and plastic products	-4.8	-38.7	-20.1	7.5	4.1	14.4	3.6	16.2	9.0
DI	Other non-metallic mineral products	-12.9	-17.0	-1.2	-11.7	5.0	6.9	3.2	8.2	2.0
DJ	Basic metals and fabricated metal products	-1.4	-34.0	-2.6	-7.2	2.3	12.4	-2.4	4.1	1.6
DK	Machinery and equipment n.e.c.	-3.9	-32.6	-38.1	-17.3	-5.4	9.6	1.5	15.1	0.0
DL	Electrical and optical equipment	4.6	-48.0	-8.7	-9.3	9.7	21.5	6.4	24.6	9.9
DM	Transport equipment	-12.4	-35.8	-6.2	-3.5	-14.3	23.5	26.4	16.3	8.5
DN	Manufacturing n.e.c.	-12.1	-13.8	17.5	-12.7	-7.2	10.6	8.5	4.6	0.3

Table B.1.2 Czech Republic—Employment Growth
(Annual changes in percent)

		1990	1991	1992	1993	1994	1995	1996	1997	1993-97
D	Manufacturing total	-8.1	-10.7	-13.2	-7.0	-5.0	-2.4	-3.4	-2.5	-4.1
DA	Food products; beverages and tobacco	-4.1	-12.5	-17.1	-0.2	0.5	0.1	1.3	1.4	0.6
DB	Textiles and textile products	-5.9	-15.2	-13.5	-6.4	-6.0	-5.5	-8.0	-3.4	-5.9
DC	Leather and leather products	-0.8	-16.2	-18.7	-5.3	-6.4	-5.4	-9.4	-12.9	-7.9
DD	Wood and wood products	-11.8	-9.2	-20.1	-3.6	-3.1	-1.2	-4.7	-2.9	-3.1
DE	Pulp, paper & paper products; publishing & printing	-14.2	1.4	3.8	-6.7	-2.2	-2.5	-2.5	-2.2	-3.2
DF	Coke, refined petroleum products & nuclear fuel	0.0	-5.6	4.9	-3.3	-11.0	-6.9	-1.3	0.0	-4.6
DG	Chemicals, chemical products and man-made fibres	-8.5	-1.5	21.2	-7.9	-3.7	-0.4	-4.8	-6.1	-4.6
DH	Rubber and plastic products	-2.5	-15.8	-10.4	11.6	2.2	2.9	-0.5	4.8	4.1
DI	Other non-metallic mineral products	-14.0	-3.1	-29.7	-3.9	-3.2	-2.7	-4.7	-3.8	-3.7
DJ	Basic metals and fabricated metal products	-2.9	-10.5	3.7	-7.7	-5.1	-1.4	-2.6	-3.4	-4.1
DK	Machinery and equipment n.e.c.	-8.4	-8.1	-36.1	-10.5	-8.6	-4.8	-6.4	-5.8	-7.2
DL	Electrical and optical equipment	10.7	-19.4	2.0	-11.2	-2.7	1.2	-1.0	-2.7	-3.4
DM	Transport equipment	-25.4	-14.4	-16.5	-9.7	-8.0	-3.7	0.1	-1.1	-4.6
DN	Manufacturing n.e.c.	-9.5	-2.8	56.1	-7.1	-7.1	-2.5	-3.0	5.0	-3.0

Table B.1.3 Czech Republic—Average Monthly Gross Wages (EUC)
(Annual changes in percent)

		1990	1991	1992	1993	1994	1995	1996	1997	1993-97
D	Manufacturing total	-25.4	-26.9	20.0	33.7	16.3	16.5	17.0	8.2	18.1
DA	Food products; beverages and tobacco	-25.3	-23.4	23.9	32.3	14.7	16.0	18.2	7.8	17.5
DB	Textiles and textile products	-25.7	-30.5	16.0	29.7	14.4	14.0	15.3	7.1	15.9
DC	Leather and leather products	-24.8	-31.7	13.8	27.1	13.3	11.9	13.5	2.7	13.4
DD	Wood and wood products	-24.3	-29.1	20.7	30.5	14.0	15.6	15.0	7.2	16.2
DE	Pulp, paper & paper products; publishing & printing	-24.8	-24.3	24.2	36.2	20.4	16.9	19.2	8.5	19.9
DF	Coke, refined petroleum products & nuclear fuel	-25.6	-21.4	15.1	27.8	17.5	21.5	15.8	14.9	19.4
DG	Chemicals, chemical products and man-made fibres	-25.1	-26.1	23.7	35.5	19.4	16.4	18.2	8.4	19.3
DH	Rubber and plastic products	-24.7	-25.2	13.3	40.0	14.7	16.4	17.5	7.5	18.7
DI	Other non-metallic mineral products	-23.7	-25.0	29.0	30.9	16.1	16.4	16.1	9.5	17.6
DJ	Basic metals and fabricated metal products	-25.0	-25.7	22.0	34.4	15.1	17.1	15.0	6.5	17.3
DK	Machinery and equipment n.e.c.	-25.9	-27.8	13.4	34.2	17.2	16.5	16.2	10.1	18.6
DL	Electrical and optical equipment	-26.0	-28.4	23.3	36.2	16.4	17.5	17.7	8.4	18.9
DM	Transport equipment	-25.7	-28.2	22.1	38.6	19.0	17.0	20.2	10.9	20.8
DN	Manufacturing n.e.c.	-23.6	-27.1	18.3	30.0	16.2	15.1	15.6	6.6	16.4

Sources: National statistics and WIIW estimates.

Table B.1.4 Czech Republic—Labor Productivity
(Annual changes in percent)

		1990	1991	1992	1993	1994	1995	1996	1997	1993-97
D	Manufacturing total	3.0	-19.0	4.8	-1.6	5.1	11.3	8.3	9.2	6.4
DA	Food products; beverages and tobacco	0.7	16.4	7.3	-4.9	-2.3	4.1	3.1	3.2	0.6
DB	Textiles and textile products	4.0	-19.6	8.4	-9.0	3.9	6.6	2.9	1.6	1.1
DC	Leather and leather products	-1.0	-14.0	-8.3	3.3	3.4	-5.3	3.4	-13	-1.9
DD	Wood and wood products	-2.5	-7.6	7.3	-14.1	4.2	4.0	2.4	6.5	0.3
DE	Pulp, paper & paper products; publishing & printing	10.4	-14.8	10.1	-1.7	21.7	4.4	-2.1	14.5	7.0
DF	Coke, refined petroleum products & nuclear fuel	-11.8	-31.7	-15.2	-5.0	21.3	15.0	7.9	11	9.7
DG	Chemicals, chemical products and man-made fibres	2.2	-27.4	23.4	0.5	6.4	-0.6	17.2	7.1	5.9
DH	Rubber and plastic products	-2.3	-27.1	-10.8	-3.7	1.9	11.2	4.1	11.6	4.9
DI	Other non-metallic mineral products	1.3	-14.4	40.7	-8.1	8.5	9.9	8.3	12.6	6.0
DJ	Basic metals and fabricated metal products	1.6	-26.2	-6.1	0.5	7.8	14.0	0.2	7.7	5.9
DK	Machinery and equipment n.e.c.	5.0	-26.7	-3.2	-7.6	3.5	15.1	8.4	22.1	7.8
DL	Electrical and optical equipment	-5.5	-35.5	-10.5	2.1	12.7	20.1	7.4	28.4	13.8
DM	Transport equipment	17.4	-25.0	12.3	6.9	-6.8	28.2	26.3	17	13.5
DN	Manufacturing n.e.c.	-2.8	-11.4	-24.8	-6.0	-0.1	13.4	11.8	-1.1	3.3

Table B.1.5 Czech Republic—Unit Labor Costs (ECU)
(Annual changes in percent)

		1990	1991	1992	1993	1994	1995	1996	1997	1993-97
D	Manufacturing total	-27.5	-9.8	14.5	35.8	10.6	4.7	8.1	-0.9	11.0
DA	Food products; beverages and tobacco	-25.8	-34.2	15.5	39.1	17.4	11.5	14.6	4.5	16.9
DB	Textiles and textile products	-28.5	-13.6	7.0	42.5	10.0	6.9	12.0	5.5	14.7
DC	Leather and leather products	-24.1	-20.6	24.0	23.1	9.5	18.1	9.8	18.1	15.6
DD	Wood and wood products	-22.3	-23.3	12.5	52.0	9.4	11.1	12.3	0.6	15.8
DE	Pulp, paper & paper products; publishing & printing	-31.9	-11.1	12.8	38.6	-1.1	12.0	21.7	-5.3	12.1
DF	Coke, refined petroleum products & nuclear fuel	-15.6	15.0	35.8	34.4	-3.2	5.6	7.3	3.5	8.8
DG	Chemicals, chemical products and man-made fibres	-26.7	1.8	0.3	34.8	12.2	17.2	0.9	1.2	12.8
DH	Rubber and plastic products	-22.9	2.7	27.1	45.3	12.6	4.7	12.8	-3.6	13.2
DI	Other non-metallic mineral products	-24.7	-12.4	-8.3	42.4	7.0	6.0	7.2	-2.7	11.0
DJ	Basic metals and fabricated metal products	-26.2	0.7	29.9	33.7	6.8	2.8	14.8	-1.1	10.7
DK	Machinery and equipment n.e.c.	-29.4	-1.5	17.2	45.2	13.2	1.2	7.3	-9.8	10.0
DL	Electrical and optical equipment	-21.6	11.1	37.7	33.4	3.2	-2.1	9.6	-15.5	4.5
DM	Transport equipment	-36.8	-4.3	8.6	29.7	27.7	-8.7	-4.8	-5.2	6.4
DN	Manufacturing n.e.c.	-21.3	-17.8	57.2	38.4	16.3	1.4	3.4	7.8	12.7

Table B.1.6 Czech Republic—Direct and Indirect Labor Costs
(1996 in percent)

		Direct	Indirect
		labor costs	
D	Manufacturing total	71.3	28.7
DA	Food products; beverages and tobacco	70.7	29.3
DB	Textiles and textile products	72.4	27.6
DC	Leather and leather products	72.8	27.2
DD	Wood and wood products	72.4	27.6
DE	Pulp, paper & paper products; publishing & printing	71.9	28.1
DF	Coke, refined petroleum products & nuclear fuel	70.1	29.9
DG	Chemicals, chemical products and man-made fibres	69.9	30.1
DH	Rubber and plastic products	71.7	28.3
DI	Other non-metallic mineral products	70.4	29.6
DJ	Basic metals and fabricated metal products	71.4	28.6
DK	Machinery and equipment n.e.c.	71.6	28.4
DL	Electrical and optical equipment	71.6	28.4
DM	Transport equipment	70.8	29.2
DN	Manufacturing n.e.c.	71.7	28.3

Sources: National statistics and WIIW estimates.

Table B.2.1 Hungary—Production Growth
(Annual changes in percent)

		1990	1991	1992	1993	1994	1995	1996	1997	1993-97
			UNIDO -Data							
D	Manufacturing total	-10.7	-16.7	-17.4	3.4	9.6	7.1	3.7	22.6	9.0
DA	Food products; beverages and tobacco	-2.7	-2.8	-13.2	-4.2	5.5	2.4	-0.1	-7.2	-0.8
DB	Textiles and textile products	-15.8	-23.8	-20.2	2.7	4.1	-1.3	-2.9	0.2	0.5
DC	Leather and leather products	-13.8	-16.4	-24.1	1.6	4.7	-11.0	-7.9	12.8	-0.3
DD	Wood and wood products	-2.8	-4.2	-8.1	5.7	16.1	0.8	-4.6	4.6	4.3
DE	Pulp, paper & paper products; publishing & printing	-7.9	-11.4	-7.7	7.5	-0.5	7.7	-9.0	20.4	4.8
DF	Coke, refined petroleum products & nuclear fuel	-3.2	-13.3	1.3	-2.0	2.6	1.7	-6.6	-6.6	-2.3
DG	Chemicals, chemical products and man-made fibres	-14.1	-22.9	-24.1	0.6	2.7	-2.2	-6.0	6.7	0.3
DH	Rubber and plastic products	3.5	-5.6	-8.9	12.2	28.2	6.0	1.8	13.7	12.0
DI	Other non-metallic mineral products	-2.4	-26.1	-10.8	10.7	3.8	5.9	1.1	4.4	5.1
DJ	Basic metals and fabricated metal products	-12.2	-30.0	-24.8	14.0	19.7	7.7	-0.9	8.3	9.5
DK	Machinery and equipment n.e.c.	-13.1	-8.8	-20.4	-3.3	9.6	13.6	-2.8	-0.2	3.2
DL	Electrical and optical equipment	-15.5	-23.0	-27.1	12.1	33.3	14.6	54.9	98.9	39.5
DM	Transport equipment	-29.0	-26.3	-35.7	28.6	14.9	51.1	27.1	63.6	35.9
DN	Manufacturing n.e.c.	-21.3	-14.3	-27.8	6.7	-3.6	4.2	-10.7	-0.6	-1.0

Table B.2.2 Hungary—Employment Growth
(Annual changes in percent)

		1990	1991	1992	1993	1994	1995	1996	1993-96
			UNIDO-Data						
D	Manufacturing total	-4.6	-9.9	-14.5	-12.9	-9.1	-4.0	-2.9	-5.8
DA	Food products; beverages and tobacco	-2.0	-3.5	-4.7	-15.8	-8.4	-7.8	-5.8	-8.7
DB	Textiles and textile products	-7.4	-14.5	-10.2	-8.6	-5.5	-6.8	-1.9	-4.5
DC	Leather and leather products	-7.3	2.6	-12.8	-9.6	-22.0	-4.3	-0.2	-6.1
DD	Wood and wood products	2.5	0.0	-4.9	-17.4	-3.6	0.6	-9.1	-7.3
DE	Pulp, paper & paper products; publishing & printing	3.0	-2.9	-12.1	-7.3	-8.7	-5.3	-10.5	-7.3
DF	Coke, refined petroleum products & nuclear fuel	0.0	0.0	266.7	-5.3	-12.0	-4.0	-5.8	-7.0
DG	Chemicals, chemical products and man-made fibres	0.0	-7.9	-10.3	-5.7	-6.3	-2.9	-3.6	-5.5
DH	Rubber and plastic products	-3.7	0.0	-19.2	-9.9	-2.5	2.7	5.3	0.8
DI	Other non-metallic mineral products	-3.5	-9.1	-20.0	-11.6	-10.0	-1.2	-3.0	-5.4
DJ	Basic metals and fabricated metal products	-8.1	-14.9	-22.7	-10.0	-10.5	-0.9	-7.0	-6.2
DK	Machinery and equipment n.e.c.	4.6	-8.1	-26.4	-23.9	-13.9	-6.2	-2.1	-9.0
DL	Electrical and optical equipment	-9.9	-20.7	-26.9	-16.2	-5.5	-4.1	5.2	-0.1
DM	Transport equipment	-9.5	-9.0	-19.7	-9.4	-12.2	-7.1	3.4	-2.4
DN	Manufacturing n.e.c.	-14.3	-16.7	-23.3	-12.6	-12.5	-6.7	-4.1	-8.8

Table B.2.3 Hungary—Average Monthly Gross Wages (ECU)
(Annual changes in percent)

		1990	1991	1992	1993	1994	1995	1996	1993-96
			UNIDO-Data						
D	Manufacturing total	0.0	9.5	14.5	18.4	6.4	-6.6	3.7	6.2
DA	Food products; beverages and tobacco	0.7	8.8	13.1	21.3	6.1	-8.2	2.1	5.5
DB	Textiles and textile products	-2.0	9.0	11.4	11.3	2.1	-6.5	3.8	4.0
DC	Leather and leather products	-0.9	2.4	5.6	13.4	6.7	-8.7	3.7	4.4
DD	Wood and wood products	-0.5	5.7	11.8	13.6	5.1	-7.4	0.0	3.5
DE	Pulp, paper & paper products; publishing & printing	5.5	7.6	11.6	15.9	5.5	-9.3	-0.1	4.7
DF	Coke, refined petroleum products & nuclear fuel	7.1	26.4	1.7	20.6	5.8	-5.9	6.1	7.4
DG	Chemicals, chemical products and man-made fibres	-2.3	13.5	14.7	20.5	10.3	-4.7	7.5	9.2
DH	Rubber and plastic products	-2.1	-1.2	11.6	14.5	4.8	-5.8	2.5	5.2
DI	Other non-metallic mineral products	7.2	8.9	13.8	18.5	6.4	-6.1	3.6	6.5
DJ	Basic metals and fabricated metal products	-0.5	7.3	12.8	16.9	9.9	-6.5	1.6	6.5
DK	Machinery and equipment n.e.c.	-2.8	7.5	13.1	18.8	7.2	-6.0	3.3	6.6
DL	Electrical and optical equipment	0.1	15.6	14.6	16.7	5.7	-6.5	4.9	5.8
DM	Transport equipment	-2.3	9.2	13.4	25.9	6.8	-3.7	10.0	10.2
DN	Manufacturing n.e.c.	-3.5	7.8	11.4	16.7	2.8	-11.6	4.3	4.4

Sources: National statistics and WIIW estimates.

Table B.2.4 Hungary—Labor Productivity
(Annual changes in percent)

		1990	1991	1992	1993	1994	1995	1996	1993-96
D	Manufacturing total				18.6	20.5	11.6	6.9	15.7
DA	Food products; beverages and tobacco				13.7	15.1	11.0	6.0	8.6
DB	Textiles and textile products				12.3	10.1	5.9	-1.0	5.3
DC	Leather and leather products				12.4	34.2	-7.0	-7.7	6.2
DD	Wood and wood products				28.0	20.5	0.2	5.0	12.5
DE	Pulp, paper & paper products; publishing & printing				15.9	9.0	13.8	1.7	13.0
DF	Coke, refined petroleum products & nuclear fuel				3.5	16.5	5.9	-0.8	5.1
DG	Chemicals, chemical products and man-made fibres				6.7	9.6	0.7	-2.5	6.1
DH	Rubber and plastic products				24.6	31.5	3.2	-3.4	11.2
DI	Other non-metallic mineral products				25.2	15.3	7.2	4.2	11.2
DJ	Basic metals and fabricated metal products				26.6	33.7	8.7	6.6	16.8
DK	Machinery and equipment n.e.c.				27.1	27.3	21.1	-0.7	13.4
DL	Electrical and optical equipment				33.9	41.1	10.0	47.3	39.6
DM	Transport equipment				41.9	30.9	62.8	22.8	39.2
DN	Manufacturing n.e.c.				22.0	10.2	11.6	-6.9	8.6

Table B.2.5 Hungary—Unit Labor Costs (ECU)
(Annual changes in percent)

		1990	1991	1992	1993	1994	1995	1996	1993-96
D	Manufacturing total				-0.2	-11.7	-16.3	-3.0	-8.2
DA	Food products; beverages and tobacco				6.7	-7.8	-17.3	-3.7	-2.9
DB	Textiles and textile products				-0.9	-7.3	-11.7	4.8	-1.2
DC	Leather and leather products				0.9	-20.5	-1.9	12.4	-1.7
DD	Wood and wood products				-11.2	-12.8	-7.5	-4.7	-8.0
DE	Pulp, paper & paper products; publishing & printing				-0.1	-3.2	-20.3	-1.8	-7.3
DF	Coke, refined petroleum products & nuclear fuel				16.6	-9.2	-11.2	7.0	2.2
DG	Chemicals, chemical products and man-made fibres				13.0	0.7	-5.3	10.2	3.0
DH	Rubber and plastic products				-8.1	-20.3	-8.7	6.0	-5.4
DI	Other non-metallic mineral products				-5.3	-7.8	-12.4	-0.5	-4.2
DJ	Basic metals and fabricated metal products				-7.7	-17.8	-13.9	-4.7	-8.8
DK	Machinery and equipment n.e.c.				-6.6	-15.8	-22.4	4.0	-5.9
DL	Electrical and optical equipment				-12.9	-25.1	-15.1	-28.8	-24.2
DM	Transport equipment				-11.3	-18.4	-40.9	-10.4	-20.8
DN	Manufacturing n.e.c.				-4.3	-6.7	-20.8	12.0	-3.9

Table B.2.6 Hungary—Direct and Indirect Labor Costs, 1995–97
(In percent)

		1995		1996		1997	
		Direct labor costs	Indirect labor costs	Direct labor costs	Indirect labor costs	Direct labor costs	Indirect labor costs
D	Manufacturing total	57.2	42.8	57.8	42.2	58.9	41.1
DA	Food products; beverages and tobacco	58.2	41.8	58.2	41.8	59.1	40.9
DB	Textiles and textile products	58.6	41.4	60.0	40.0	60.2	39.8
DC	Leather and leather products	58.1	41.9	61.1	38.9	60.7	39.3
DD	Wood and wood products	58.3	41.7	57.9	42.1	58.7	41.3
DE	Pulp, paper & paper products; publishing & printing	57.4	42.6	57.8	42.2	59.4	40.6
DF	Coke, refined petroleum products & nuclear fuel	.	.	52.4	47.6	55.2	44.8
DG	Chemicals, chemical products and man-made fibres	56.1	43.9	56.2	43.8	58.1	41.9
DH	Rubber and plastic products	57.3	42.7	58.7	41.3	59.6	40.4
DI	Other non-metallic mineral products	58.2	41.8	58.1	41.9	59.3	40.7
DJ	Basic metals and fabricated metal products	58.2	41.8	57.6	42.4	63.8	36.2
DK	Machinery and equipment n.e.c.	53.9	46.1	57.4	42.6	58.5	41.5
DL	Electrical and optical equipment	56.4	43.6	58.2	41.8	59.2	40.8
DM	Transport equipment	58.3	41.7	59.1	40.9	60.1	39.9
DN	Manufacturing n.e.c.	58.4	41.6	59.6	40.4	59.8	40.2

Sources: National statistics and WIIW estimates.

Table B.3.1 Poland—Production Growth
(Annual changes in percent)

		1990	1991	1992	1993	1994	1995	1996	1997	1993-97
			UNIDO -Data							
D	Manufacturing total	-25.6	-13.2	3.9	10.2	14.0	11.8	9.8	13.3	11.8
DA	Food products; beverages and tobacco	-24.7	-0.2	5.5	9.0	12.7	8.9	9.0	9.4	9.8
DB	Textiles and textile products	-37.9	-17.7	3.0	9.1	12.8	0.6	3.8	9.8	7.1
DC	Leather and leather products	-34.9	-20.8	-10.6	-1.2	12.6	8.3	12.5	4.2	7.1
DD	Wood and wood products	-25.1	30.4	15.4	3.7	10.6	10.0	12.7	12.0	9.8
DE	Pulp, paper & paper products; publishing & printing	-24.2	-5.4	7.5	24.8	13.6	17.7	12.5	16.9	17.0
DF	Coke, refined petroleum products & nuclear fuel	-24.4	-14.8	12.4	12.3	7.2	5.6	2.8	1.7	5.9
DG	Chemicals, chemical products and man-made fibres	-25.9	-12.7	-0.2	6.1	17.3	13.1	4.9	11.9	10.6
DH	Rubber and plastic products	-26.4	8.0	13.9	19.9	16.1	17.0	17.2	21.1	18.2
DI	Other non-metallic mineral products	-27.5	-8.3	8.5	9.8	14.6	4.8	9.5	11.9	10.1
DJ	Basic metals and fabricated metal products	-23.8	-19.6	-2.9	3.7	16.3	15.5	7.7	13.6	11.2
DK	Machinery and equipment n.e.c.	-21.3	-24.0	-10.5	9.4	15.5	20.9	9.8	8.7	12.8
DL	Electrical and optical equipment	-21.2	-20.8	0.1	16.5	13.9	19.1	15.5	20.6	17.1
DM	Transport equipment	-24.8	-37.0	19.0	19.4	17.4	9.7	18.2	24.6	17.8
DN	Manufacturing n.e.c.	-45.9	-28.0	-5.6	8.9	13.9	24.1	11.9	24.8	16.5

Table B.3.2 Poland—Employment Growth
(Annual changes in percent)

		1990	1991	1992	1993	1994	1995	1996	1997	1993-97
			UNIDO-Data							
D	Manufacturing total	-9.4	-11.4	-13.1	-2.4	-0.3	4.3	-0.2	0.7	0.4
DA	Food products; beverages and tobacco	-2.9	-0.7	-3.0	1.4	-2.5	6.4	0.4	2.1	1.5
DB	Textiles and textile products	-12.2	-14.6	-17.1	0.9	1.8	7.3	-5.8	-3.0	0.1
DC	Leather and leather products	-15.8	-18.8	-17.6	-9.3	-4.1	-1.3	0.3	9.6	-1.2
DD	Wood and wood products	-13.9	-1.4	-7.9	-1.4	1.1	13.5	6.8	0.7	4.0
DE	Pulp, paper & paper products; publishing & printing	-8.9	-12.2	-15.3	-2.6	5.3	5.4	3.8	8.0	3.9
DF	Coke, refined petroleum products & nuclear fuel	0.0	0.0	-20.7	0.9	0.9	-0.8	-0.4	-1.3	-0.2
DG	Chemicals, chemical products and man-made fibres	-7.9	-11.7	-5.6	-2.6	3.4	0.5	-1.0	-2.6	-0.5
DH	Rubber and plastic products	-6.3	-5.3	-15.5	7.8	10.9	4.3	7.1	8.6	7.7
DI	Other non-metallic mineral products	-5.0	-7.6	-13.3	-2.6	-4.5	3.6	-0.2	1.4	-0.5
DJ	Basic metals and fabricated metal products	-9.0	-8.6	-9.1	-3.5	-2.0	3.7	5.2	-0.8	0.5
DK	Machinery and equipment n.e.c.	-10.0	-13.7	-17.0	-5.1	-4.2	0.4	-4.2	-3.4	-3.3
DL	Electrical and optical equipment	-7.8	-20.9	-22.7	-8.7	-0.2	0.4	-1.2	1.4	-1.7
DM	Transport equipment	-8.3	-14.9	-12.8	-8.1	1.4	-2.3	-1.8	-2.2	-2.7
DN	Manufacturing n.e.c.	-31.1	-32.3	-42.9	1.5	4.4	15.2	2.1	7.1	5.9

Table B.3.3 Poland—Average Monthly Gross Wages (ECU)
(Annual changes in percent)

		1990	1991	1992	1993	1994	1995	1996	1997	1993-97
			UNIDO-Data							
D	Manufacturing total	-38.1	52.9	2.6	13.8	8.1	14.9	18.2	11.1	13.2
DA	Food products; beverages and tobacco	-38.9	60.5	3.0	7.0	4.7	14.7	19.3	11.5	11.3
DB	Textiles and textile products	-42.6	53.0	1.5	11.1	4.5	8.6	12.8	9.1	9.2
DC	Leather and leather products	-44.6	54.6	0.2	10.4	5.1	14.4	17.6	8.5	11.1
DD	Wood and wood products	39.8	52.7	3.4	10.9	8.7	12.4	14.9	9.3	11.2
DE	Pulp, paper & paper products; publishing & printing	-37.6	63.8	4.2	13.4	8.2	19.4	19.7	12.9	14.6
DF	Coke, refined petroleum products & nuclear fuel	-26.2	48.9	1.6	29.4	10.6	17.1	10.9	4.1	14.1
DG	Chemicals, chemical products and man-made fibres	-35.5	46.4	4.5	20.0	15.6	20.6	20.7	11.6	17.6
DH	Rubber and plastic products	-38.2	60.9	7.8	17.3	9.1	16.5	12.3	9.3	12.8
DI	Other non-metallic mineral products	-37.8	57.8	1.5	13.7	12.0	16.6	18.1	13.3	14.7
DJ	Basic metals and fabricated metal products	-33.9	50.1	-1.2	13.9	9.3	16.7	18.0	10.1	13.5
DK	Machinery and equipment n.e.c.	-37.7	46.8	1.6	15.0	7.5	16.3	19.5	12.0	14.0
DL	Electrical and optical equipment	-39.3	51.9	3.2	23.1	9.2	15.0	19.2	13.8	15.9
DM	Transport equipment	-36.4	45.1	7.4	19.4	8.7	14.0	20.1	13.6	15.1
DN	Manufacturing n.e.c.	-41.9	65.3	-13.9	10.2	5.3	11.8	14.8	9.9	10.4

Sources: National statistics and WIIW estimates.

Table B.3.4 Poland—Labor Productivity
(Annual changes in percent)

		1993	1994	1995	1996	1997	1993-97
D	Manufacturing total	12.9	14.3	7.2	10.1	12.5	11.4
DA	Food products; beverages and tobacco	7.5	15.5	2.3	8.6	7.2	8.1
DB	Textiles and textile products	8.2	10.8	-6.3	10.2	13.2	7.0
DC	Leather and leather products	8.9	17.4	9.7	12.2	-4.9	8.4
DD	Wood and wood products	5.1	9.5	-3.0	5.5	11.2	5.5
DE	Pulp, paper & paper products; publishing & printing	28.1	7.8	11.7	8.3	8.2	12.6
DF	Coke, refined petroleum products & nuclear fuel	11.3	6.3	6.5	3.3	3.0	6.0
DG	Chemicals, chemical products and man-made fibres	8.9	13.5	12.5	5.9	14.9	11.1
DH	Rubber and plastic products	11.2	4.7	12.2	9.4	11.5	9.8
DI	Other non-metallic mineral products	12.7	20.0	1.2	9.7	10.3	10.6
DJ	Basic metals and fabricated metal products	7.5	18.6	11.3	2.4	14.5	10.7
DK	Machinery and equipment n.e.c.	15.3	20.7	20.4	14.6	12.5	16.7
DL	Electrical and optical equipment	27.6	14.1	18.7	16.9	18.9	19.2
DM	Transport equipment	30.0	15.8	12.2	20.4	27.3	21.0
DN	Manufacturing n.e.c.	7.3	9.1	7.7	9.7	16.5	10.0

Table B.3.5 Poland—Unit Labor Costs (ECU)
(Annual changes in percent)

		1993	1994	1995	1996	1997	1993-97
D	Manufacturing total	0.8	-5.4	7.3	7.3	-1.3	1.6
DA	Food products; beverages and tobacco	-0.5	-9.3	12.1	9.8	4.1	3.0
DB	Textiles and textile products	2.7	-5.6	15.9	2.4	-3.6	2.1
DC	Leather and leather products	1.4	-10.4	4.3	4.8	14.1	2.5
DD	Wood and wood products	5.5	-0.7	15.9	8.9	-1.7	5.4
DE	Pulp, paper & paper products; publishing & printing	-11.5	0.4	6.9	10.4	4.4	1.8
DF	Coke, refined petroleum products & nuclear fuel	16.2	4.0	10.0	7.4	1.1	7.6
DG	Chemicals, chemical products and man-made fibres	10.2	1.8	7.1	14.0	-2.8	5.9
DH	Rubber and plastic products	5.5	4.3	3.8	2.6	-2.0	2.8
DI	Other non-metallic mineral products	0.9	-6.7	15.3	7.7	2.7	3.7
DJ	Basic metals and fabricated metal products	6.0	-7.9	4.8	15.3	-3.9	2.5
DK	Machinery and equipment n.e.c.	-0.2	-10.9	-3.4	4.3	-0.5	-2.3
DL	Electrical and optical equipment	-3.5	-4.3	-3.1	1.9	-4.3	-2.7
DM	Transport equipment	-8.1	-6.1	1.6	-0.3	-10.8	-4.9
DN	Manufacturing n.e.c.	2.7	-3.5	3.9	4.7	-5.7	0.3

Table B.3.6 Poland—Direct and Indirect Labor Costs
(1996 in percent)

		Direct labor	Indirect costs
D	Manufacturing total	69.8	30.2
DA	Food products; beverages and tobacco	70.1	29.9
DB	Textiles and textile products	71.1	28.9
DC	Leather and leather products	70.0	30.0
DD	Wood and wood products	69.5	30.5
DE	Pulp, paper & paper products; publishing & printing	70.2	29.8
DF	Coke, refined petroleum products & nuclear fuel	69.1	30.9
DG	Chemicals, chemical products and man-made fibres	71.0	29.0
DH	Rubber and plastic products	71.2	28.8
DI	Other non-metallic mineral products	68.8	31.2
DJ	Basic metals and fabricated metal products	68.5	31.6
DK	Machinery and equipment n.e.c.	70.1	29.9
DL	Electrical and optical equipment	71.3	28.7
DM	Transport equipment	69.2	30.8
DN	Manufacturing n.e.c.	70.1	29.9

Sources: National statistics and WIIW estimates.

Table B.4.1 Slovenia—Production Growth
(Annual changes in percent)

		1990	1991	1992	1993	1994	1995	1996	1997	1993-97
D	Manufacturing total	-9.1	-10.9	-13.8	-3.9	6.3	2.3	-0.5	-2.7	0.2
DA	Food products; beverages and tobacco	1.3	-4.5	-17.3	-3.5	2.7	-0.2	5.4	-3.0	0.2
DB	Textiles and textile products	-13.4	-15.3	-14.0	1.0	-4.0	2.8	-3.4	0.0	-0.8
DC	Leather and leather products	-16.1	-18.2	1.5	-4.7	-3.8	-11.7	-19.4	11.9	-6.1
DD	Wood and wood products	-9.9	-14.0	-12.1	-1.6	6.6	-0.7	0.9	-27.7	-5.3
DE	Pulp, paper & paper products; publishing & printing	-5.0	-6.1	-12.1	-5.1	10.0	-6.6	-2.8	-11.6	-3.5
DF	Coke, refined petroleum products & nuclear fuel	11.9	9.3	-0.5	0.0	-32.8	35.9	-23.4	9.2	-5.2
DG	Chemicals, chemical products and man-made fibres	-11.9	-13.0	-27.0	-2.0	15.7	3.2	3.4	3.8	4.7
DH	Rubber and plastic products	-3.5	-4.0	-12.0	3.0	7.3	5.5	-1.7	14.1	5.5
DI	Other non-metallic mineral products	-7.7	-13.3	33.3	-5.0	12.0	1.0	6.3	4.8	3.7
DJ	Basic metals and fabricated metal products	-9.4	-17.1	-7.8	-5.0	6.6	5.0	-5.6	-3.7	-0.7
DK	Machinery and equipment n.e.c.	-8.0	-1.0	-20.6	-5.0	17.8	3.1	-6.9	-11.5	-1.0
DL	Electrical and optical equipment	-23.7	-15.2	-17.0	2.0	21.0	16.9	16.4	-3.0	10.3
DM	Transport equipment	-6.5	-16.7	-16.5	-16.0	-2.7	4.4	-7.1	-7.8	-6.1
DN	Manufacturing n.e.c.	-18.2	-8.2	-6.0	4.0	3.5	-5.4	0.2	16.4	3.5

Table B.4.2 Slovenia—Employment Growth
(Annual changes in percent)

		1990	1991	1992	1993	1994	1995	1996	1997	1993-97
D	Manufacturing total	-4.1	-11.6	-10.1	-9.0	-4.7	-5.1	-5.5	-4.0	-5.7
DA	Food products; beverages and tobacco	-1.3	-5.3	-8.6	-7.8	0.5	0.3	-1.0	-1.5	-1.9
DB	Textiles and textile products	-5.3	-8.9	-8.6	-3.0	-4.0	-8.0	-9.9	-7.3	-6.5
DC	Leather and leather products	1.6	-11.7	-9.6	-6.9	-7.2	-10.9	-10.4	-3.6	-7.8
DD	Wood and wood products	-8.4	-9.8	-10.7	-5.7	-3.7	-7.4	-2.8	-5.4	-5.0
DE	Pulp, paper & paper products; publishing & printing	-2.6	-7.4	-7.6	-7.5	-1.4	-1.6	-3.4	-3.5	-3.5
DF	Coke, refined petroleum products & nuclear fuel	-5.4	-6.4	-55.8	-0.4	-9.3	-15.9	-4.7	-8.6	-7.9
DG	Chemicals, chemical products and man-made fibres	0.9	-10.6	-10.7	-11.9	4.3	-0.2	0.1	1.5	-1.4
DH	Rubber and plastic products	-6.8	0.3	-1.6	-5.0	-4.0	-2.7	-0.9	-1.3	-2.8
DI	Other non-metallic mineral products	-0.5	-11.4	-16.5	-6.2	-3.8	3.4	1.1	-8.8	-3.0
DJ	Basic metals and fabricated metal products	-4.6	-12.7	-10.6	-17.5	-7.5	-16.7	-4.7	-5.3	-10.5
DK	Machinery and equipment n.e.c.	-3.5	-11.7	-14.4	-5.4	-10.4	4.5	-4.9	-0.5	-3.5
DL	Electrical and optical equipment	-7.2	-15.9	-8.5	-11.1	-4.7	-4.3	-4.7	-3.1	-5.6
DM	Transport equipment	0.8	-17.8	-9.5	-12.7	-6.0	-7.6	-14.0	-13.2	-10.7
DN	Manufacturing n.e.c.	-9.1	-19.1	-10.2	-9.2	-5.0	2.3	-9.6	3.7	-3.7

Table B.4.3 Slovenia—Average Monthly Gross Wages (ECU)
(Annual changes in percent)

		1992	1993	1994	1995	1996	1997	1993-97
D	Manufacturing total	-4.8	14.6	10.2	16.5	3.2	5.3	9.8
DA	Food products; beverages and tobacco	-10.8	20.5	9.3	15.9	1.9	2.2	9.7
DB	Textiles and textile products	-1.9	12.4	4.0	12.2	-0.1	3.8	6.3
DC	Leather and leather products	0.3	8.0	4.0	13.1	0.2	5.7	6.1
DD	Wood and wood products	-4.1	17.5	7.7	15.1	2.5	4.9	9.4
DE	Pulp, paper & paper products; publishing & printing	-4.6	16.7	5.0	14.5	4.2	5.4	9.0
DF	Coke, refined petroleum products & nuclear fuel	-13.5	-0.7	1.0	37.3	0.3	6.7	8.1
DG	Chemicals, chemical products and man-made fibres	-6.3	23.0	14.0	18.8	5.4	5.0	13.0
DH	Rubber and plastic products	0.5	12.0	7.3	17.7	-0.1	2.6	7.7
DI	Other non-metallic mineral products	-1.9	14.3	10.2	14.8	3.0	5.6	9.5
DJ	Basic metals and fabricated metal products	-5.4	11.5	15.8	18.0	3.6	6.4	10.9
DK	Machinery and equipment n.e.c.	-1.3	11.2	12.3	16.9	2.3	6.2	9.7
DL	Electrical and optical equipment	-4.3	16.3	14.0	15.9	4.0	6.1	11.2
DM	Transport equipment	-8.0	13.5	10.3	18.8	4.4	5.7	10.4
DN	Manufacturing n.e.c.	-8.8	16.5	7.0	17.5	1.6	5.0	9.3

Sources: National statistics and WIIW estimates.

49

Table B.4.4 Slovenia—Labor Productivity
(Annual changes in percent)

		1990	1991	1992	1993	1994	1995	1996	1997	1993-97
D	Manufacturing total	-5.7	0.4	-4.3	5.8	12.0	8.5	6.2	1.9	6.8
DA	Food products; beverages and tobacco	2.6	0.9	-9.5	4.6	2.2	-0.5	6.5	-1.6	2.2
DB	Textiles and textile products	-8.5	-7.0	-6.0	4.1	0.0	11.7	10.5	7.9	6.8
DC	Leather and leather products	-17.5	-7.3	12.2	2.3	3.6	-0.9	-10.1	16.1	1.9
DD	Wood and wood products	-1.7	-5.1	-1.6	4.4	10.7	7.3	3.8	-23.5	-0.3
DE	Pulp, paper & paper products; publishing & printing	-2.4	1.4	-4.9	2.5	11.5	-5.1	0.6	-8.4	0.0
DF	Coke, refined petroleum products & nuclear fuel	18.3	16.8	125.0	0.4	-25.9	61.5	-19.7	19.5	2.9
DG	Chemicals, chemical products and man-made fibres	-12.7	-2.6	-18.3	11.2	11.0	3.4	3.3	2.3	6.2
DH	Rubber and plastic products	3.6	-4.3	-10.6	8.4	11.8	8.4	-0.9	15.6	8.5
DI	Other non-metallic mineral products	-7.3	-2.2	59.6	1.2	16.4	-2.3	5.2	14.9	6.8
DJ	Basic metals and fabricated metal products	-5.1	-5.0	3.1	15.1	15.2	26.0	-1.0	1.7	11.0
DK	Machinery and equipment n.e.c.	-4.7	12.1	-7.2	0.4	31.5	-1.3	-2.1	-11.1	2.6
DL	Electrical and optical equipment	-17.8	0.8	-9.2	14.7	27.0	22.2	22.2	0.1	16.8
DM	Transport equipment	-7.2	1.3	-7.7	-3.8	3.5	13.0	8.0	6.2	5.2
DN	Manufacturing n.e.c.	-10.0	13.5	4.7	14.6	9.0	-7.5	10.9	12.2	7.5

Table B.4.5 Slovenia—Unit Labor Costs (ECU)
(Annual changes in percent)

		1992	1993	1994	1995	1996	1997	1993-97
D	Manufacturing total	-0.5	8.3	-1.6	7.3	-2.8	3.3	2.8
DA	Food products; beverages and tobacco	-1.3	15.2	6.9	16.4	-4.3	3.8	7.3
DB	Textiles and textile products	4.3	8.0	4.1	0.4	-9.6	-3.9	-0.4
DC	Leather and leather products	-10.6	5.5	0.3	14.1	11.4	-9.0	4.2
DD	Wood and wood products	-2.6	12.5	-2.7	7.3	-1.2	37.2	9.7
DE	Pulp, paper & paper products; publishing & printing	0.3	13.9	-5.8	20.6	3.5	15.0	9.0
DF	Coke, refined petroleum products & nuclear fuel	-61.5	-1.1	36.4	-15.0	24.9	-10.7	5.0
DG	Chemicals, chemical products and man-made fibres	14.7	10.6	2.8	14.9	2.1	2.7	6.5
DH	Rubber and plastic products	12.4	3.4	-4.0	8.6	0.7	-11.3	-0.8
DI	Other non-metallic mineral products	-38.6	12.9	-5.3	17.5	-2.1	-8.1	2.5
DJ	Basic metals and fabricated metal products	-8.2	-3.1	0.5	-6.4	4.6	4.6	-0.1
DK	Machinery and equipment n.e.c.	6.3	10.8	-14.6	18.5	4.5	19.4	6.9
DL	Electrical and optical equipment	5.4	1.4	-10.3	-5.1	-14.8	6.0	-4.9
DM	Transport equipment	-0.3	17.9	6.5	5.2	-3.4	-0.5	4.9
DN	Manufacturing n.e.c.	-12.9	1.7	-1.9	27.0	-8.3	-6.4	1.7

Employment: in enterprises, companies and organizations;

1989-96: private enterprises are included only if they have 3 or more persons in paid employment and armed forces staff.

From 1997: including private enterprises with 1 and 2 employees.

Wages: in enterprises, companies and organizations.

Sources: National statistics and WIIW estimates.

Annex C

Table C.1 Czech Republic—Gaining and Losing Industries in Exports to the European Union(12), 1993–97

	NACE	Exports 1997 ECU mn	Average annual change in %	Competitive gain,1993-97 ECU mn	Market share in the EU(12) 1997 in %
30 biggest winners					
Manuf.& assembly of motor vehicles & mot.v.eng.	351	791.9	30.6	426.1	2.90
Manuf.of electrical mach.(compr.electr.motors,etc)	342	674.1	37.1	410.6	4.42
Manuf.of tools&finished met.goods(exc.electr.equ)	316	605.6	38.3	377.5	5.99
Manufacture of other machinery and equipment	328	416.0	52.7	311.9	1.88
Manuf. of parts and access. for motor vehicles	353	386.8	64.1	309.2	6.01
Processing of plastics	483	255.9	38.0	161.7	2.76
Manufacture of insulated wires and cables	341	233.0	43.1	149.1	6.50
Manuf.of electrical apparatus,batteries,accumul.	343	150.7	56.9	114.4	1.71
Production and prel. processing of n-ferr.metals	224	246.1	22.8	110.1	0.87
Manufacture of rubber products	481	216.1	24.3	93.3	4.52
Manufacture of petrochemicals	252	415.9	14.5	76.2	1.86
Manuf.of plant f.mines,iron&steel ind.&foundries	325	181.4	20.5	71.2	3.22
Manuf.of radio, tv receiving sets, sound reprod,...	345	114.7	36.1	70.4	0.35
Manufacture of machine-tools for working metal	322	180.6	23.0	68.4	3.60
Manuf. of mach. for the food, chem.,related ind.	324	99.7	38.8	65.4	2.36
Manuf.of structural met.prod.(incl.integr.assembly)	314	170.3	14.5	55.6	12.74
Foundries	311	99.3	32.7	54.8	9.92
Sawing and processing of wood	461	123.0	20.1	53.0	1.80
Manufacture of ceramic goods	248	122.6	21.8	51.9	6.86
Manufacture of textile machinery and accessoires	323	87.2	31.3	51.2	6.05
Yarns	43A	69.4	38.8	44.4	2.22
Woven fabrics	43B	179.0	12.9	42.9	3.55
Printing and allied industries	473	73.6	28.7	42.4	3.07
Manufacture of telecommunications equipment	344	67.4	40.0	42.2	0.34
Manuf.of oth.mach.&equip.f.use in spec.br.of ind.	327	66.8	33.7	41.8	2.29
Manuf.of transmission equipment f. motive power	326	78.8	31.2	41.4	2.65
Manufacture of steel tubes	222	98.3	23.7	40.7	5.12
Manuf.of optical instruments & photogr. equip.	373	54.8	49.1	40.3	0.84
Miscellaneous manufacturing industries	495	181.3	17.4	36.2	0.71
Manufacture of toys and sport goods	494	82.0		32.1	1.03
5 biggest losers					
Extraction of building materials & refractory clays	231	26.8	-8.9	-13.1	2.07
Manuf.of ready-made clothing and accessories)	453	277.8	3.5	-14.8	1.22
Iron & steel industry (as def. in ECSC Treaty)	221	244.7	6.7	-24.0	3.46
Manuf.of mass-prod.footwear (excl.wood,rubber)	451	103.5	-1.0	-34.7	1.55
Manufacture of cement, lime and plaster	242	53.5	-11.1	-43.8	12.43
Total		9691.8	21.6	3888.5	1.68

Note: Market shares without intra-EU trade.
Sources: National statistics and WIIW estimates.

51

Table C.2 Hungary—Gaining and Losing Industries in Exports to the European Union(12), 1993–97

	NACE	Exports 1997 ECU mn	Average annual change in %	Competitive gain, 1993-97 ECU mn	Market share in the EU(12) 1997 in %
30 biggest winners					
Manuf.& assembly of motor vehicles & mot.v.eng.	351	1580.2	104.8	1459.4	5.78
Manuf. office mach.and data-processing mach.	330	714.9	121.4	672.4	1.63
Manuf.of radio, tv receiving sets, sound reprod,...	345	609.1	81.1	533.9	1.84
Manuf.of electrical mach.(compr.electr.motors,etc)	342	441.6	43.1	296.0	2.90
Manuf. of parts and access. for motor vehicles	353	258.0	61.2	202.4	4.01
Production and prel. processing of n-ferr.metals	224	265.5	25.9	132.6	0.94
Manufacture of other machinery and equipment	328	232.2	32.2	128.6	1.05
Manufacture of insulated wires and cables	341	343.5	23.7	122.2	9.58
Manufacture of domestic type electric appliances	346	173.1	27.6	93.6	5.26
Manuf.of electr.lamps & oth.eletr. lighting equip.	347	192.9	24.7	86.9	10.22
Iron & steel industry (as def. in ECSC Treaty)	221	132.7	31.4	69.3	1.88
Manuf.of electrical apparatus,batteries,accumul.	343	101.1	39.2	61.9	1.15
Manuf.of tools&finished met.goods(exc.electr.equ)	316	208.2	17.5	57.3	2.06
Manufacture of telecommunications equipment	344	61.8	43.5	40.8	0.31
Processing of plastics	483	105.1	20.7	39.0	1.13
Knitting industry	436	244.3	10.2	34.4	1.66
Manufacture of rubber products	481	95.9	20.5	34.2	2.00
Manuf.of mass-prod.footwear (excl.wood,rubber)	451	242.7	10.1	31.1	3.64
Manufacture of agricult. machinery and tractors	321	74.4	20.6	27.0	3.86
Manuf.of structural met.prod.(incl.integr.assembly)	314	75.1	15.7	26.5	5.62
Manuf. of oth. chem. prod. chiefly for household	259	39.0	35.7	26.2	1.05
Manuf.of carpentry and joinery components	463	44.6	24.6	22.7	2.86
Miscellaneous manufacturing industries	495	90.9	19.3	22.6	0.36
Manufacture of toys and sport goods	494	50.2	21.3	21.7	0.63
Manuf. of mach. for the food, chem.,related ind.	324	51.7	20.5	20.4	1.22
Manufacture of other basic chemicals	253	55.8	20.4	20.4	0.67
Manuf.of standard and narrow-gauge railway	362	22.1	58.8	18.2	5.19
Manufacture of pulp, paper and board	471	25.8	39.5	17.3	0.15
Manufacture of semi-finished wood products	462	26.5	30.9	15.6	1.01
Manuf.of plant f.mines,iron&steel ind.&foundries	325	86.4	11.5	14.9	1.53
5 biggest losers					
Manufacture of glass and glassware	247	59.5	0.6	-14.3	2.47
Manufacture of wooden furniture	467	71.5	-1.7	-20.9	1.79
Processing and preserving of fruit and vegetables	414	73.5	-0.4	-21.3	1.66
Manuf.of ready-made clothing and accessoires)	453	526.1	3.8	-22.9	2.31
Slaughtering, preparing and preseving of meat	412	357.4	2.5	-40.5	6.93
Total		8984.9	26.4	4384.1	1.55

Note: Market shares without intra-EU trade.
Sources: WIIW calculation based on Eurostat COMEXT database.

Table C.3 Poland—Gaining and Losing Industries in Exports to the European Union(12), 1993–97

	NACE	Exports 1997 ECU mn	Average annual change in %	Competitive gain,1993–97 ECU mn	Market share in the EU(12) 1997 in %
30 biggest winners					
Manuf.of radio, tv receiving sets, sound reprod,...	345	449.0	65.4	369.4	1.36
Manuf.& assembly of motor vehicles & mot.v.eng.	351	892.7	19.7	307.2	3.27
Manuf.of tools&finished met.goods(exc.electr.equ)	316	505.4	32.9	281.7	5.00
Manufacture of wooden furniture	467	762.7	15.4	244.7	19.06
Manuf.of electrical mach.(compr.electr.motors,etc)	342	288.6	43.0	193.2	1.89
Manuf. of parts and access. for motor vehicles	353	210.3	60.7	164.4	3.27
Production and prel. processing of n-ferr.metals	224	704.7	11.9	140.0	2.51
Iron & steel industry (as def. in ECSC Treaty)	221	339.7	24.4	137.5	4.80
Manufacture of other machinery and equipment	328	228.4	28.1	112.9	1.03
Manuf.of carpentry and joinery components	463	146.0	33.8	92.0	9.37
Manufacture of insulated wires and cables	341	193.3	29.2	88.8	5.39
Processing of plastics	483	164.8	30.4	88.5	1.78
Manuf.of structural met.prod.(incl.integr.assembly)	314	231.5	14.7	76.7	17.31
Manuf.of electrical apparatus,batteries,accumul.	343	106.7	49.1	75.3	1.21
Manufacture of pulp, paper and board	471	157.0	24.0	74.3	0.92
Other wood manufactures (except furniture)	465	285.1	18.2	74.3	19.49
Manufacture of other basic chemicals	253	263.5	16.3	71.4	3.19
Knitting industry	436	307.8	13.2	70.1	2.09
Processing of paper and board	472	94.8	44.2	67.6	2.52
Manuf.of electr.lamps & oth.electr. lighting equip.	347	142.6	24.8	64.6	7.56
Manufacture of telecommunications equipment	344	88.7	44.1	59.2	0.44
Manufacture of petrochemicals	252	293.3	14.9	57.2	1.31
Manuf.of household text.&oth.made-up text.goods	455	149.3	19.8	55.6	5.58
Manufacture of rubber products	481	147.7	21.2	54.9	3.09
Manuf.of ready-made clothing and accessoires)	453	1341.7	5.8	46.9	5.88
Processing and preserving of fruit and vegetables	414	317.1	10.1	43.4	7.17
Manufacture of glass and glassware	247	124.8	17.4	41.4	5.19
Manufacture of agricult. machinery and tractors	321	74.2	31.5	40.7	3.84
Foundries	311	95.0	24.0	39.2	9.49
Manufacture of ceramic goods	248	81.1	23.2	36.4	4.54
5 biggest losers					
Slaughtering, preparing and preseving of meat	412	154.6	2.3	-18.9	3.00
Sawing and processing of wood	461	137.2	-2.1	-39.7	2.01
Process.&preserv.of fish&oth.sea foods f.hum.con	415	86.2	-4.7	-45.2	2.13
Aerospace equipment manufact. and repairing	364	13.3	-31.5	-61.2	0.06
Shipbuilding	361	43.4	-28.8	-104.3	1.52
Total		**11897.9**	**16.0**	**3514.4**	**2.06**

Note: Market shares without intra-EU trade.
Sources: WIIW calculation based on Eurostat COMEXT database.

Table C.4 Slovenia—Gaining and Losing Industries in Exports to the European Union(12), 1993–97

	NACE	Exports 1997 ECU millions	Average annual change in %	Competitive gain,1993-97 ECU millions	Market share in the EU(12) 1997 in %
30 biggest winners					
Manuf.& assembly of motor vehicles & mot.v.eng.	351	580.1	20.4	208.4	2.12
Manuf.of tools&finished met.goods(exc.electr.equ)	316	308.7	28.0	149.8	3.05
Production and prel. processing of n-ferr.metals	224	200.5	21.6	85.3	0.71
Manuf.of electrical mach.(compr.electr.motors,etc)	342	190.6	15.7	43.7	1.25
Manufacture of domestic type electric appliances	346	222.5	9.9	36.4	6.77
Manuf. of parts and access. for motor vehicles	353	88.8	21.7	29.8	1.38
Manuf.of plant f.mines,iron&steel ind.&foundries	325	64.1	21.0	25.9	1.14
Manuf.of electrical apparatus,batteries,accumul.	343	85.4	18.8	22.9	0.97
Manufacture of petrochemicals	252	52.8	25.0	22.4	0.24
Manufacture of other machinery and equipment	328	122.9	12.3	17.8	0.55
Iron & steel industry (as def. in ECSC Treaty)	221	57.2	18.0	15.2	0.81
Woven fabrics	43B	50.6	15.1	15.0	1.00
Manufacture of glass and glassware	247	44.2	15.1	12.2	1.84
Manufacture of other basic chemicals	253	53.4	13.5	10.4	0.65
Manufacture of machine-tools for working metal	322	31.1	20.5	10.1	0.62
Manuf.of measuring, checking & prec.instr.& app.	371	33.0	14.9	8.8	0.91
Manufacture of toys and sport goods	494	27.6	15.3	8.4	0.35
Forging:drop forging,closed dieforg.,press.&stamp.	312	15.4	33.5	8.2	2.08
Manuf.of radio, tv receiving sets, sound reprod,...	345	31.6	15.2	7.8	0.10
Manufacture of clocks & watches & parts there	374	9.1	63.7	7.6	0.27
Processing of plastics	483	54.2	11.2	6.8	0.59
Manuf.of transmission equipment f. motive power	326	19.0	20.9	6.5	0.64
Man-made fibres industry	260	28.4	15.8	6.4	1.35
Secondary transformation, treatm.&coating of met.	313	19.3	19.2	5.8	1.06
Production of grindstones & other abravise prod.	246	15.6	16.3	5.3	3.90
Manuf. of mach. for the food, chem.,related ind.	324	25.3	12.2	4.9	0.60
Manuf.of medical & surgical equip.& orthop.appl.	372	11.2	24.6	4.9	0.25
Shipbuilding	361	7.0	23.2	4.3	0.24
Manuf.of electr.lamps & oth.eletr. lighting equip.	347	13.3	18.2	4.3	0.71
Manufacture of furs and of fur goods	456	4.1	40.8	2.7	1.14
5 biggest losers					
Manufacture of rubber products	481	68.8	-2.2	-33.2	1.44
Manuf.of mass-prod.footwear (excl.wood,rubber)	451	66.3	-4.5	-35.6	0.99
Manufacture of wooden furniture	467	113.3	-5.1	-54.9	2.83
Knitting industry	436	102.1	-6.9	-70.1	0.69
Manuf.of ready-made clothing and accessoires)	453	333.9	-1.4	-94.4	1.46
Total		3961.4	9.0	321.5	0.69

Note: Market shares without intra-EU trade.
Sources: WIIW calculation based on Eurostat COMEXT database.

Annex D

Table D.1 Czech Republic—Revealed Comparative Advantage Values

	NACE	1993	1994	1995	1996	1997	RCA improvement 97/96 over 93/94 in %
				RCA Values			
Manufacture of insulated wires and cables	341	-8.83	30.07	48.95	49.30	61.10	419.791
Manuf.of cycles, motor-cycles & parts & access.	363	-5.25	30.95	23.86	57.06	65.58	377.308
Manuf.of transmission equipment f. motive power	326	1.62	9.76	34.40	32.05	12.57	291.943
Manufacture of toys and sport goods	494	15.29	25.45	18.03	45.15	49.13	131.385
Man-made fibres industry	260	7.53	5.03	-20.30	-12.63	40.29	120.074
Manuf.of art.of cork,straw,oth.plainting materials	466	11.12	22.21	4.36	32.50	39.77	116.854
Production and prel. processing of non-ferr.metals	224	5.88	21.20	25.10	24.80	29.84	101.763
Manuf. of parts and access. for motor vehicles	353	22.36	27.83	40.75	47.42	43.70	81.559
Manuf.of tools&finished met.goods(exc.electr.equ)	316	27.66	35.13	42.77	55.64	48.96	66.570
Woven fabrics	43B	5.48	6.91	15.84	6.60	13.47	62.010
Manuf.of art.of jewellery,gold & silversmith's ware	491	16.41	21.27	10.45	34.01	17.11	35.654
Manufacture of clocks & watches & parts thereof	374	20.82	43.39	38.24	38.69	46.75	33.039
Other wood manufactures (except furniture)	465	209.73	132.58	200.12	211.62	172.05	12.087
Foundries	311	90.33	143.30	136.63	137.26	119.76	10.015
Manufacture of ceramic goods	248	31.31	15.87	18.06	23.50	27.06	7.169
Manufacture of wooden furniture	467	101.89	100.10	101.12	104.18	108.24	5.163
Shipbuilding	361	294.34	77.90	51.13	159.92	231.35	5.112
Photographic, cinematographic laboratories	493	-87.69	-27.47	-61.56	21.48	93.71	0.030
Sugar manufacturing and refining	420	87.73	77.00	-57.95	-6.42	170.54	-0.368
Manufacture of wooden containers	464	310.62	242.08	278.55	302.92	235.83	-2.524
Manufacture of pharmaceutical products	257	-205.86	-218.87	-223.55	-189.84	-225.07	-197.686
Production of grindstones & other abravise prod.	246	-52.66	-57.01	-58.23	-52.83	-56.92	-200.085
Manuf.of carpets,linoleum and oth.floor coverings	438	-184.91	-205.29	-226.38	-208.21	-194.22	-203.135
Manuf. of oth.chem.prod.,mainly f.ind.&agricult.pur.	256	-150.20	-171.23	-161.78	-167.19	-170.16	-204.954
Manufacture of other food products	423	-198.51	-235.63	-200.65	-243.12	-260.64	-216.039
Processing and preserving of fruit and vegetables	414	-63.94	-104.33	-99.77	-103.42	-91.83	-216.039
Process.&preserv.of fish&oth.sea foods f.hum.con	415	-453.16	-543.39	-502.19	-532.49	-701.94	-223.871
Manufacture of tobacco products	429	-456.32	-504.85	-490.26	-560.27	-640.67	-224.945
Manuf.of animal and poultry foods (incl.fish meal)	422	-183.08	-221.55	-256.26	-230.76	-276.97	-225.480
Maufacture of vegetable and animal oils and fats	411	-56.03	-55.64	-67.18	-62.61	-96.20	-242.216
Distilling of ethyl alcohol from fermented materials	424	-266.04	-248.55	-351.29	-436.72	-405.68	-263.703
Grain milling	416	-102.99	-89.16	-355.67	-194.70	-136.30	-272.263
Manufacture of domestic type electric appliances	346	-44.19	-73.33	-112.28	-120.23	-108.13	-294.316
Manufacture of starch and starch products	418	-466.66	118.98	0.00	-374.00	-386.26	-318.667
Extract. and preparat. of non-ferr. metal ores	212	127.14	13.15	-7.83	-143.82	-199.96	-345.053
Tanning and dressing of leather	441	-27.43	-48.18	-88.74	-109.88	-103.99	-382.859
Manuf.& assembly of motor vehicles & mot.v.eng.	351	13.05	-30.39	-44.47	-44.99	-7.30	-401.674
Other mineral extraction	239	26.84	-5.68	-13.60	-61.28	-67.59	-708.816
Manufacture of agricult. machinery and tractors	321	4.73	-12.27	-15.28	-46.94	-30.29	-1124.099
Manufacture of dairy products	413	4.14	-5.64	-43.74	-25.48	-1.06	-1866.012

Sources: National statistics and WIIW estimates.

Table D.2 Hungary—Revealed Comparative Advantage Values

	NACE	1993	1994	1995	1996	1997	RCA improvement 97/96over 93/94 in %
				RCA VALUES			
Sugar manufacturing and refining	420	-122.57	-56.77	182.47	337.81	277.64	243.165
Manufacture of toys and sport goods	494	-12.66	-1.87	-9.09	22.33	17.21	172.252
Grain milling	416	-82.29	-25.29	170.77	59.95	154.85	99.670
Manufacture of wooden containers	464	87.75	28.15	9.82	84.72	139.70	93.641
Manuf.of radio, tv receiving sets, sound reproduction	345	-47.19	3.02	39.40	34.53	44.83	79.663
Manuf. of parts and access. for motor vehicles	353	13.50	64.06	66.55	70.19	55.05	61.491
Manufacture of other basic chemicals	253	15.42	32.91	41.61	47.04	25.71	50.537
Manuf.of structural met.prod.(incl.integr.assembly)	314	32.02	41.81	21.54	50.38	58.65	47.682
Manuf.& assembly of motor vehicles & mot.v.eng.	351	-112.98	-34.63	77.75	88.37	109.35	33.944
Manufacture of domestic type electric appliances	346	62.76	59.17	41.59	74.19	73.33	20.993
Manuf.of carpentry and joinery components	463	151.25	217.87	219.12	221.64	211.29	17.288
Slaughtering, preparing and preserving of meat	412	211.53	158.50	176.42	224.14	187.65	11.285
Manuf.of household text.& other made-up text.goods	455	163.67	152.57	136.52	173.17	143.71	0.204
Other wood manufactures (except furniture)	465	144.91	81.02	135.11	91.83	127.83	-2.777
Manuf.of prod.from leather & leather substitutes	442	113.74	98.70	88.62	105.62	94.01	-6.032
Manuf.of mass-prod.footwear (excl. wood, rubber)	451	106.30	89.75	89.85	90.01	89.06	-8.664
Iron & steel industry (as def. in ECSC Treaty)	221	19.12	121.22	73.80	85.04	41.33	-9.952
Manuf. of electr.lamps & oth. electrical lighting equip.	347	161.23	178.34	145.02	154.49	147.77	-10.988
Manuf.of bodies for motor vehicles	352	62.66	67.52	103.43	58.77	55.88	-11.940
Manuf.of ready-made clothing and accessoires	453	185.20	175.99	152.79	155.00	162.38	-12.129
Manuf.of soft drinks,incl.bottling of nat.spa waters	428	-154.55	-132.72	-256.52	-180.33	-233.88	-244.187
Manuf.of animal and poultry foods (incl.fish meal)	422	-81.07	-106.55	-119.16	-105.48	-165.53	-244.450
Manufacture of pulp, paper and board	471	-120.02	-73.39	-168.11	-175.28	-135.72	-260.798
Secondary transformation, treatm.&coating of met.	313	-107.50	-98.74	-103.42	-153.38	-183.09	-263.146
Yarns	43A	-29.06	-20.84	-15.59	-39.12	-43.22	-264.989
Forging:drop forging,closed dieforg.,press.&stamp.	312	-65.17	-65.89	-42.93	-102.97	-114.49	-265.930
Processing of plastics	483	-72.99	-63.11	-97.23	-119.72	-106.52	-266.228
Boilermaking, manuf.of reserv.,tanks,sheet-met c.	315	-35.41	-89.08	-54.50	-96.63	-113.62	-268.890
Miscellaneous manufacturing industries	495	-65.72	-73.11	-71.52	-48.21	-194.31	-274.684
Manufacture of cement, lime and plaster	242	-311.29	-203.92	-527.40	-438.25	-474.19	-277.102
Manuf.of tools&finished met.goods(exc.electr.equ)	316	7.72	2.83	2.04	-1.37	-18.28	-286.255
Other mineral extraction	239	17.09	52.55	3.18	-52.71	-121.84	-350.666
Manuf.of transmission equipment f. motive power	326	-26.28	-49.20	-78.16	-108.85	-119.56	-402.615
Manufacture of other food products	423	-4.03	-30.58	-73.26	-53.75	-54.41	-412.469
Manuf.of plant f.mines,iron&steel ind.&foundries	325	-2.22	-12.74	-18.14	-34.16	-14.09	-422.416
Manuf. of clay prod. for constructional purposes	241	73.82	-44.95	-19.52	-61.87	-79.38	-589.286
Man-made fibres industry	260	-15.02	-1.59	-48.76	-71.30	-10.01	-589.446
Extract. and preparat. of non-ferr. metal ores	212	-44.05	-3.02	-91.13	-136.71	-123.40	-652.531
Manuf.of art.of cork,straw,oth.plainting materials	466	0.56	6.79	-11.94	-41.06	-59.85	-1472.439
Manufacture of clocks & watches & parts thereof	374	-11.17	1.15	-29.62	-140.39	-170.43	-3202.530

Sources: National statistics and WIIW estimates.

Table D.3 Poland—Revealed Comparative Advantage Values

	Nace	1993	1994	1995	1996	1997	RCA improvement 97/96 over 93/94 in %
				RCA VALUES			
Man-made fibres industry	260	-1.42	3.93	10.07	-27.28	68.41	1534.281
Manufacture of dairy products	413	8.54	8.22	45.70	115.20	87.09	1106.989
Drawing, cold rolling and cold folding of steel	223	-9.59	2.22	8.69	11.93	25.54	408.706
Slaughtering, preparing and preserving of meat	412	51.33	-19.82	13.65	46.36	54.94	221.488
Manuf.of tools&finished met.goods(exc.electr.equ)	316	3.98	16.52	32.12	32.65	31.66	213.619
Manuf.of transmission equipment f. motive power	326	10.13	17.75	29.95	46.40	26.36	160.967
Manufacture of rubber products	481	12.75	20.63	28.95	40.23	41.50	144.845
Manufacture of furs and of fur goods	456	67.42	81.45	100.44	189.57	151.68	129.222
Manufacture of musical instruments	492	22.23	15.58	30.47	33.73	40.19	95.459
Other means of transport	365	47.34	89.36	120.98	119.52	145.07	93.568
Manufacture of toys and sport goods	494	-11.06	-18.14	-1.67	24.74	25.96	73.645
Knitting industry	436	42.09	29.90	28.26	48.37	51.30	38.437
Foundries	311	94.00	115.51	126.47	140.89	130.87	29.713
Manufacture of insulated wires and cables	341	98.60	102.32	147.92	141.96	115.72	28.252
Manuf.of household text.&oth.made-up text.goods	455	186.42	212.03	231.85	233.77	239.70	18.827
Other wood manufactures (except furniture)	465	313.83	262.67	325.43	328.28	339.43	15.821
Manufacture of other basic chemicals	253	86.73	97.58	109.70	109.26	104.03	15.724
Processing and preserving of fruit and vegetables	414	205.08	174.16	198.92	226.61	206.67	14.250
Iron & steel industry (as def. in ECSC Treaty)	221	72.05	126.32	124.01	99.36	121.77	11.476
Manuf.of electr.lamps & oth.eletr. lighting equip.	347	81.41	97.69	86.18	96.81	101.56	10.761
Manuf.of optical instruments & photogr. equip.	373	-225.30	-204.31	-227.08	-201.77	-214.19	-196.823
Manufacture of starch and starch products	418	-300.00	-444.65	-162.69		-724.62	-197.310
Manufacture of ceramic goods	248	-51.30	-52.49	-59.93	-47.74	-53.56	-197.608
Manufacture of textile machinery and accessoires	323	-186.61	-192.92	-191.94	-187.50	-192.02	-199.996
Manuf.of paint, painter's fillings, varnish, print.ink	255	-465.11	-444.90	-511.26	-491.36	-465.24	-205.119
Manuf.of oth.mach.&equip.f.use in spec.br.of ind.	327	-190.97	-211.24	-220.22	-228.21	-198.59	-206.116
Manufacture of pharmaceutical products	257	-263.38	-306.82	-356.23	-295.12	-327.96	-209.272
Manuf.of wine of fresh grapes&bev.based thereon	425	-567.16	-704.21	0.00	-668.32	-857.11	-219.983
Manuf. of oth.chem.prod.,mainly f.ind.&agricult.pur.	256	-162.70	-183.82	-203.83	-229.06	-219.59	-229.472
Manuf.& assembly of motor vehicles & mot.v.eng.	351	-9.79	1.55	-4.43	-13.64	2.22	-238.588
Grain milling	416	-302.91	-458.65	-280.74	-501.14	-667.93	-253.509
Retreading and repairing of rubber tyres	482	78.27	2.67	-72.09	-72.93	-55.89	-259.145
Miscellaneous manufacturing industries	495	-19.95	-82.03	-30.31	-113.81	-62.15	-272.546
Manufacture of agricult. machinery and tractors	321	26.51	15.90	-2.60	-42.63	-43.59	-303.308
Manufacture of domestic type electric appliances	346	-16.17	-62.48	-82.42	-87.63	-77.50	-309.932
Boilermaking, manuf.of reserv.,tanks,sheet-met c.	315	26.07	-14.34	-7.51	-5.97	-22.70	-344.390
Manuf.of bodies for motor vehicles	352	-20.06	-39.69	-83.47	-97.99	-153.26	-520.518
Tanning and dressing of leather	441	2.10	-20.12	-41.01	-69.01	-65.14	-844.204
Manuf.of standard and narrow-gauge railway	362	71.75	-48.82	6.54	-151.90	-62.90	-1036.715
Manufacture of steel tubes	222	-5.18	9.52	-1.42	-21.06	-33.79	-1364.319

Sources: National statistics and WIIW estimates.

Table D.4 Slovenia—Revealed Comparative Advantage Values

	NACE	1993	1994	1995	1996	1997	RCA improvement 97/96 over 93/94 in %
				RCA Values			
Slaughtering, preparing and preserving of meat	412	25.33	-30.76	-19.99	38.74	60.59	1729.616
Manuf.of standard and narrow-gauge railway	362	81.53	-69.05	-202.53	-113.22	203.02	619.888
Manufacture of toys and sport goods	494	12.67	11.83	25.73	14.57	40.72	125.694
Man-made fibres industry	260	-33.76	-23.71	28.74	32.69	59.79	60.925
Production and prel. processing of n-ferr.metals	224	55.30	66.37	72.50	87.83	92.22	47.983
Production of grindstones & other abravise prod.	246	73.23	60.52	80.84	83.06	114.24	47.509
Other wood manufactures (except furniture)	465	188.27	58.12	175.26	162.59	173.28	36.312
Manuf.of tools&finished met.goods(exc.electr.equ)	316	63.60	80.18	75.39	77.41	93.91	19.154
Manufacture of furs and of fur goods	456	-89.29	-20.79	-29.68	59.47	68.06	15.857
Manuf.of bodies for motor vehicles	352	99.49	68.03	68.73	93.57	90.90	10.117
Sawing and processing of wood	461	152.23	122.29	151.62	133.42	165.76	8.982
Manufacture of domestic type electric appliances	346	142.68	133.74	159.20	157.80	133.21	5.278
Manuf.of electrical mach.(compr.electr.motors,etc)	342	73.07	63.75	61.25	68.09	63.67	-3.693
Manufacture of other basic chemicals	253	-44.49	-1.26	0.98	43.83	0.10	-3.987
Manuf.of ready-made clothing and accessoires	453	213.61	194.94	185.53	184.11	181.62	-10.481
Manufacture of pulp, paper and board	471	80.87	105.16	120.46	91.09	68.11	-14.423
Manuf.of concrete,cement or plast.prod.f.const.	243	71.23	69.76	102.85	89.29	25.47	-18.600
Foundries	311	129.30	123.99	110.80	103.46	99.10	-20.026
Manuf.of soft drinks,incl.bottling of nat.spa waters	428	80.88	70.28	30.76	56.67	63.82	-20.290
Manufacture of semi-finished wood products	462	33.68	78.01	43.29	49.18	30.74	-28.446
Manufacture of ceramic goods	248	-73.07	-91.76	-83.95	-95.44	-107.47	-223.104
Other mineral extraction	239	-110.02	-194.77	-145.24	-186.48	-190.80	-223.783
Manuf. of oth.chem.prod.,mainly f.ind.&agricult.pur.	256	-158.07	-143.50	-187.87	-193.48	-185.66	-225.722
Manuf.of carpets,linoleum and oth.floor coverings	438	-195.62	-182.35	-188.23	-247.80	-249.64	-231.607
Processing of plastics	483	-75.31	-72.66	-87.60	-93.87	-106.81	-235.615
Manufacture of agricult. machinery and tractors	321	-69.71	-103.51	-139.93	-124.04	-111.45	-235.949
Manuf. of soap, synth. detergents, perfume	258	-222.54	-211.87	-300.38	-288.57	-338.24	-244.294
Miscellaneous manufacturing industries	495	-31.33	-61.57	-98.30	-61.01	-88.03	-260.424
Grain milling	416	-300.00	-489.62	-533.90	-467.38	-866.44	-268.918
Retreading and repairing of rubber tyres	482	-186.57	-201.81	-360.40	-577.49	-119.17	-279.378
Brewing and malting	427	-22.48	36.40	-3.04	8.39	-33.75	-282.290
Drawing, cold rolling and cold folding of steel	223	-31.26	-6.17	-16.29	-29.64	-39.78	-285.450
Manufacture of steel tubes	222	-86.64	-23.72	-51.32	-55.36	-167.21	-301.684
Processing and preserving of fruit and vegetables	414	-27.10	-111.63	-138.04	-160.31	-155.41	-327.574
Manufacture of telecommunications equipment	344	-1.56	16.15	16.46	-6.06	-28.03	-333.694
Manufacture of musical instruments	492	-33.73	-35.46	-93.93	-126.71	-137.75	-482.217
Manuf. of parts and access. for motor vehicles	353	27.32	4.92	-56.47	-77.18	-51.59	-499.402
Processing of paper and board	472	13.49	1.17	-17.72	-37.36	-22.06	-505.234
Manuf.of art.of jewellery,gold & silversmith´s ware	491	-0.54	-32.50	-91.90	-105.66	-168.22	-928.923
Extract. and preparat. of non-ferr. metal ores	212	16.30	35.54	-94.17	-320.53	-351.55	-1396.419

Sources: National statistics and WIIW estimates.

Annex E

Table E.1 Nominal Capital

(FIEs share in the total of the manufacturing industries, 1996, percent and percentage point change, 1994–96)

NACE-Code	Industries	Czech Republic[1] 1996	Czech Republic[1] 1994-96	Hungary 1996	Hungary 1994-96	Slovak Republic[2] 1996	Slovak Republic[2] 1995-96	Slovenia 1996	Slovenia 1995-96
DA	Food products, beverages, tobacco	29.7	13.8	66.3	2.9	21.9	2.0	12.5 [2]	7.2 [2]
DB	Textiles and textile products	4.7	2.5	51.5	8.9	26.3	7.8	2.5	0.1
DC	Leather and leather products	1.2	0.8	79.6	32.5	2.7	-1.9	*	*
DD	Wood and wood products	6.1	5.1	59.3	25.1	12.9	5.7	0.1	-0.6
DE	Pulp, paper; publishing and printing	14.7	2.0	45.8	1.0	17.3	-0.4	33.6	4.2
DF	Coke and petroleum	0.0	0.0	100.0	0.0			*	*
DG	Chemicals	14.5	9.3	83.2	30.6	14.1 [3]	-7.7 [3]	20.0	5.0
DH	Rubber and plastic	41.6	5.7	69.4	4.1	6.9	4.3	8.4	2.0
DI	Other non-metallic minerals	54.1	24.3	80.9	4.7	26.2	3.4	14.2	3.2
DJ	Basic metals	6.4	3.4	43.0	-0.3	17.1	3.1	2.4	1.5
DK	Machinery and equipment n.e.c.	5.9	2.8	56.4	11.2	16.3 [4]	6.5 [4]	18.7	1.8
DL	Electrical and optical equipment	23.0	13.4	70.9	8.4	23.3	4.0	16.3 [5]	-0.2 [5]
DM	Transport equipment	45.4	8.9	75.0	-1.3	48.5	11.7	52.8 [3]	5.4 [3]
DN	Manufacturing n.e.c.	8.7	7.2	32.6	0.4	19.1	5.3	1.6 [4]	-0.1 [4]
								13.8	1.6
D	Average in manufacturing	21.5	8.9	67.4	6.6	19.4	2.3	14.5	3.3

1) Own capital. - 2) Without tobacco. - 3) Without other transport equipment. - 4) Without recycling.
- 5) Without office machinery. * Industries with less than 3 FIEs
Source: WIIW Database on Foreign Investment Enterprises.

Table E.2 Employed Persons

(FIEs share in the total of the manufacturing industries, 1996, percent and percentage point change, 1994–96)

NACE-Code	Industries	Czech Republic 1996	Czech Republic 1994-96	Hungary 1996	Hungary 1994-96	Slovak Republic 1996	Slovak Republic 1994-96	Slovenia 1996	Slovenia 1995-96
DA	Food products, beverages, tobacco	17.3	5.9	.36.2	-3.1	11.3	0.5	7.8 [1]	2.1 [1]
DB	Textiles and textile products	8.0	4.8	28.7	-2.3	15.0	4.4	3.4	0.1
DC	Leather and leather products	3.1	1.6	39.2	4.7	6.5	1.4	*	*
DD	Wood and wood products	8.7	5.1	22.4	6.2	6.2	0.5	0.8	-0.8
DE	Pulp, paper; publishing and printing	14.5	4.5	29.5	-2.3	17.1	2.0	16.7	4.9
DF	Coke and petroleum	0.0	0.0	99.8	0.0			*	*
DG	Chemicals	8.6	5.2	69.3	23.6	20.8 [2]	3.6 [2]	12.8	2.6
DH	Rubber and plastic	31.1	7.4	34.8	-1.4	5.4	4.9	16.4	3.0
DI	Other non-metallic minerals	23.1	12.1	41.6	0.3	10.0	1.3	6.7	2.0
DJ	Basic metals	5.9	2.2	23.0	-0.5	12.4	3.1	3.8	1.5
DK	Machinery and equipment n.e.c.	6.2	2.9	20.8	-8.4	6.2 [3]	2.1 [3]	17.6	4.1
DL	Electrical and optical equipment	22.1	13.7	54.4	2.5	19.4	10.0	15.0 [2]	0.2 [2]
DM	Transport equipment	25.7	7.1	45.2	5.2	25.8	7.7	41.4 [3]	4.8 [3]
DN	Manufacturing n.e.c.	10.1	8.2	20.4	-4.8	11.3	7.4	3.3 [4]	1.2 [4]
								5.1	-1.1
D	Average in manufacturing	13.1	6.0	36.1	-1.2	13.0	3.7	10.1	1.5

1) Without tobacco. - 2) Without office machinery. - 3) Without other transport equipment. - 6) Without recycling. * Industries with less than 3 FIEs
Source: WIIW Database on Foreign Investment Enterprises.

Table E.3 Sales

(FIEs share in the total of the manufacturing industries, 1996, percent and percentage point change, 1994–96)

NACE-Code	Industries	Czech Republic		Hungary		Slovenia	
		1996	96/94	1996	96/94	1996	96/95
DA	Food products, beverages, tobacco	24.7	10.8	51.1	1.3	10.0 [1]	2.7 [1]
DB	Textiles and textile products	8.6	3.2	43.6	1.4	5.7	0.6
DC	Leather and leather products	3.9	3.2	46.1	-1.1	*	*
DD	Wood and wood products	11.5	5.9	42.6	12.7	0.9	-1.5
DE	Pulp, paper; publishing and printing	21.3	4.9	71.6	20.5	19.8	-2.8
DF	Coke and petroleum	0.0	0.0	99.2	-0.4	*	*
DG	Chemicals	11.3	6.8	78.7	25.0	17.4	3.1
DH	Rubber and plastic	43.8	6.6	54.6	-3.2	16.0	2.4
DI	Other non-metallic minerals	45.6	22.0	63.5	4.4	13.3	4.8
DJ	Basic metals	10.8	6.5	33.9	-2.6	4.6	2.5
DK	Machinery and equipment n.e.c.	8.1	4.3	45.1	3.1	21.3	0.9
DL	Electrical and optical equipment	30.7	19.8	65.1	0.7	20.1 [2]	0.0 [2]
DM	Transport equipment	55.0	11.6	84.1	12.3	82.3 [3]	10.0 [3]
DN	Manufacturing n.e.c.	28.2	25.7	30.9	0.0	5.6 [4]	2.7 [4]
						12.9	-2.5
D	Average in manufacturing	22.6	10.1	61.4	6.0	19.6	2.1

1) Without tobacco. - 2) Without office machinery. - 3) Without other transport equipment. - 4) Without recycling.
* Industries with less than 3 FIEs
Source: WIIW Database on Foreign Investment Enterprises.

Table E.4 Export Sales

(FIEs share in the total of the manufacturing industries, 1996, percent and percentage point change, 1994–96)

NACE-Code	Industries	Czech Republic		Hungary		Slovenia		Poland
		1994	94/93	1996	96/94	1996	96/95	1997
DA	Food products, beverages, tobacco	21.0	-2.3	61.2	2.3	13.4 [1]	3.4 [1]	50.0 [2]
DB	Textiles and textile products	6.0	4.6	60.0	5.2	7.3	-0.2	46.8
DC	Leather and leather products	1.5	-0.4	63.5	-1.7	*	*	38.5 [3]
DD	Wood and wood products	9.9	0.3	69.0	25.0	1.0	-2.2	31.3
DE	Pulp, paper; publishing and printing	9.9	5.0	78.0	13.7	40.3	-3.9	72.2
DF	Coke and petroleum	0.0	0.0	100.0	0.0	*	*	6.4 [4]
DG	Chemicals	6.6	0.0	89.3	35.1	17.1	4.4	22.8
DH	Rubber and plastic	54.6	21.7	60.9	-3.1	24.4	5.3	51.2
DI	Other non-metallic minerals	26.4	1.1	71.7	1.3	17.1	7.6	36.0
DJ	Basic metals	4.4	2.4	50.7	0.3	6.0	3.1	35.9
DK	Machinery and equipment n.e.c.	4.3	2.9	71.5	6.4	25.3	0.4	48.7
DL	Electrical and optical equipment	18.6	9.5	75.2	-10.0	23.2 [5]	0.1 [5]	74.0
DM	Transport equipment	58.9	0.2	90.4	12.2	86.3 [6]	5.5 [6]	68.7
DN	Manufacturing n.e.c.	4.7	2.9	55.8	0.7	5.4 [7]	1.9 [7]	39.8
						6.1	1.7	
D	Average in manufacturing	15.9	1.1	73.9	8.4	25.8	2.6	43.0

1) Without tobacco. - 2) Including agricultural products. - 3) Including raw hides and skins.- 4) Including crude oil.
5) Without office machinery. - 6) Without other transport equipment. - 7) Without recycling. * Industries with less than 3 FIEs
Source: WIIW Database on Foreign Investment Enterprises.

References

Aiginger, K., M. Peneder, and J. Stankovsky. 1994. "The Explanatory Power of Market-Based Trade Theories for the Trade Between Market Economies and Reform Countries." *Empirica* 21(2): 197–220.

Balassa, B. 1965. "Trade Liberalisation and Revealed Comparative Advantage." *The Manchester School of Economic and Social Studies* 33: 99–123.

Dietz, R. 1999. "Exchange Rates and Relative Prices in Central and Eastern European Countries: A Systems and Transaction Cost Approach." WIIW Research Reports, 254, The Vienna Institute for International Economic Studies (WIIW), Vienna, March.

Durka, B., and others. 1998. "Foreign Investments in Poland." Foreign Trade Research Institute, Warsaw.

European Bank for Reconstruction and Development (EBRD). 1998. *Transition Report 1998*, London.

European Economy. 1995. "The Interpenetration between the EU and Eastern Europe." Special supplement.

Eurostat. 1998. *Statistics in Focus*, no. 28.

Fassman, M. 1996. "We and the European Union. 2—Labor Costs and Wages." (in Czech), *Pohledy* 2–3: 1–7. Prague.

GD 3/Eurostat. 1997. "Industrial Restructuring in Central and Eastern Europe and Emerging Patterns of Industrial Specialization." In *Panorama of EU Industry* (written by WIIW), vol. 1, GD 3/Eurostat, Brussels.

Guger, A. 1996. "Internationale Lohnstückkostenposition 1995 deutlich verschlechtert." *WIFO Monatsberichte* no. 8, Austrian Institute of Economic Research, Vienna.

Gabrisch, H. 1995. "Die Integration der mittel- und osteuropäischen Länder in die europäische Wirtschaft." IWH Halle, Sonderheft 1.

Havlik, P. 1995. "Trade Reorientation and Competitiveness in CEECs." In R. Dobrinsky and M. Landesmann, eds., *Transforming Economies and European Integration*: Aldershot: Edward Elgar, 141–162.

———. 1996. "Exchange Rates, Competitiveness and Labor Costs in Central and Eastern Europe." WIIW Research Reports, no. 231, The Vienna Institute for International Economic Studies (WIIW), Vienna, October.

Havlik, P. 1997. "Trade Restructuring and Export Competitiveness." In M. Landesmann and others, *Structural Developments in Central and Eastern Europe. WIIW Report 1997*: Vienna: WIIW (December).

———. 1998. "Labour Cost Competitiveness of Central and Eastern Europe." *MOCT-MOST*, no. 2, Kluwer Academic Publishers, 13–33.

Hitchens, D., K. Wagner, J. Birnie, J. Hamar, and A. Zemplínerová. 1995. "The Comparative Productivity of Manufacturing Plants in the Czech Republic and Hungary." *Economic Systems* 19(3): 187–218.

Hu, F., and J. Sachs. 1996. "The Global Competitiveness Report 1996. Executive Summary." World Economic Forum 1996.

Hunya, G. 1998. "Integration of CEEC Manufacturing into European Corporate Structures via Direct Investment." WIIW Research Reports, no. 245, WIIW, Vienna, May.

———. 1999. "Foreign Direct Investment in CEEC Manufacturing." In M. Landesmann and others, *Structural Developments in Central and Eastern Europe. WIIW Report 1999*, WIIW, Vienna (forthcoming).

Hunya, G., and J. Stankovsky, eds. 1998. *WIIW-WIFO Database. Foreign Direct Investment in Central and East European Countries and the Former Soviet Union.* WIIW, December.

Hunya, G., and S. Richter. 1999. "Hungary: FDI, Profit Repatriation and the Current Account." *The Vienna Institute Monthly Report*, no. 3, WIIW, Vienna, March.

Krajnyak, K., and J. Zettelmeyer. 1997. "Competitiveness in Transition Economies: What Scope for Real Appreciation?" IMF Working Paper WP/97/149.

Krugman, P.R. 1994. "Competitiveness: A Dangerous Obsession." *Foreign Affairs* 73(2): 28–44.

Landesmann, M., and J. Burgstaller. 1997. "Vertical Product Differentiation in EU Markets: the Relative Position of East European Producers." WIIW Research Reports, no. 234, WIIW, Vienna, February.

———. 1999. "Trade Performance of East European Producers on EU Markets: An Assessment of Product Quality." WIIW Research Reports, no. 255, WIIW, Vienna, April (forthcoming).

Organisation for Economic Co-operation and Development (OECD). 1998. "Benchmark Results of the 1996 Eurostat-OECD Comparison by Analytical Categories," (preliminary), Paris.

Oulton, N. 1994. "Labour Productivity and Unit Labour Costs in Manufacturing: The UK and Its Competitors." *National Institute Economic Review*, May, 49–60.

Pilat, D. 1996. "Labour Productivity Levels in OECD Countries: Estimates for Manufacturing and Selected Service Sectors." Working Paper 169, OECD, Economics Department, Paris.

Pollan, W. 1997. "Große Lohnunterschiede nach Branchen in der Industrie." WIFO Monatsberichte, no. 3, Austrian Institute of Economic Research, Vienna.

Sheehy, J. 1995. "Economic Interpenetration between the European Union and Central and Eastern Europe." In R. Dobrinsky and M. Landesmann, eds., *Transforming Economies and European Integration*. Aldershot: Edward Elgar, pp. 6–80.

Taieb, H.S. 1995. "Labour Costs in a Set of Central and Western European Countries. Some Comparative Remarks." ILO-CEET Report, Budapest.

United Nations Economic Commission for Europe (UN ECE). 1998. *Economic Survey of Europe* no. 3, 88–90. UN ECE Secretariat, Geneva.

van Ark, B. 1992. "Comparative Productivity in British and American Manufacturing." *National Institute Economic Review* 142 (November): 63–73.

Wirtschaftskammer Österreich. 1998. *Die Arbeitskosten in der Industrie Österreichs 1996.* Vienna.

Wolfmayr-Schnitzer, Y., and others. 1997. "The Competitiveness of Transition Countries." WIFO-WIIW study prepared for the CCET OECD, Vienna, March.

Zemplínerová, A. 1998. "Key Determinants of Restructuring: Evidence from the Czech Manufacturing Output, Trade and Foreign Direct Investment." Paper presented at the workshop Trade between the European Union and the Associated States: Prospects for the Future, Paris, November 26.

Distributors of World Bank Group Publications

Prices and credit terms vary from country to country. Consult your local distributor before placing an order.

ARGENTINA
World Publications SA
Av. Cordoba 1877
1120 Ciudad de Buenos Aires
Tel: (54 11) 4815-8156
Fax: (54 11) 4815-8156
E-mail: wpbooks@infovia.com.ar

AUSTRALIA, FIJI, PAPUA NEW GUINEA, SOLOMON ISLANDS, VANUATU, AND SAMOA
D.A. Information Services
648 Whitehorse Road
Mitcham 3132, Victoria
Tel: (61) 3 9210 7777
Fax: (61) 3 9210 7788
E-mail: service@dadirect.com.au
URL: http://www.dadirect.com.au

AUSTRIA
Gerold and Co.
Weihburggasse 26
A-1011 Wien
Tel: (43 1) 512-47-31-0
Fax: (43 1) 512-47-31-29
URL: http://www.gerold.co/at.online

BANGLADESH
Micro Industries Development
Assistance Society (MIDAS)
House 5, Road 16
Dhanmondi R/Area
Dhaka 1209
Tel: (880 2) 326427
Fax: (880 2) 811188

BELGIUM
Jean De Lannoy
Av. du Roi 202
1060 Brussels
Tel: (32 2) 538-5169
Fax: (32 2) 538-0841

BRAZIL
Publicacões Tecnicas Internacionais Ltda.
Rua Peixoto Gomide, 209
01409 Sao Paulo, SP.
Tel: (55 11) 259-6644
Fax: (55 11) 258-6990
E-mail: postmaster@pti.uol.br
URL: http://www.uol.br

CANADA
Renouf Publishing Co. Ltd.
5369 Canotek Road
Ottawa, Ontario K1J 9J3
Tel: (613) 745-2665
Fax: (613) 745-7660
E-mail:
order.dept@renoufbooks.com
URL: http:// www.renoufbooks.com

CHINA
China Financial & Economic
Publishing House
8, Da Fo Si Dong Jie
Beijing
Tel: (86 10) 6401-7365
Fax: (86 10) 6401-7365

China Book Import Centre
P.O. Box 2825
Beijing

Chinese Corporation for Promotion
of Humanities
52, You Fang Hu Tong,
Xuan Nei Da Jie
Beijing
Tel: (86 10) 660 72 494
Fax: (86 10) 660 72 494

COLOMBIA
Infoenlace Ltda.
Carrera 6 No. 51-21
Apartado Aereo 34270
Santafé de Bogota, D.C.
Tel: (57 1) 285-2798
Fax: (57 1) 285-2798

COTE D'IVOIRE
Center d'Edition et de Diffusion
Africaines (CEDA)
04 B.P. 541
Abidjan 04
Tel: (225) 24 6510; 24 6511
Fax: (225) 25 0567

CYPRUS
Center for Applied Research
Cyprus College
6, Diogenes Street, Engomi
P.O. Box 2006
Nicosia
Tel: (357 2) 59-0730
Fax: (357 2) 66-2051

CZECH REPUBLIC
USIS, NIS Prodejna
Havelkova 22
130 00 Prague 3
Tel: (420 2) 2423 1486
Fax: (420 2) 2423 1114
URL: http://www.nis.cz/

DENMARK
SamfundsLitteratur
Rosenoerns Alle 11
DK-1970 Frederiksberg C
Tel: (45 35) 351942
Fax: (45 35) 357822
URL: http://www.sl.cbs.dk

ECUADOR
Libri Mundi
Libreria Internacional
P.O. Box 17-01-3029
Juan Leon Mera 851
Quito
Tel: (593 2) 521-606; (593 2) 544-185
Fax: (593 2) 504-209
E-mail: librimu1@librimundi.com.ec
E-mail: librimu2@librimundi.com.ec

CODEU
Ruiz de Castilla 763, Edif. Expocolor
Primer piso, Of. #2
Quito
Tel/Fax: (593 2) 507-383; 253-091
E-mail: codeu@impsat.net.ec

EGYPT, ARAB REPUBLIC OF
Al Ahram Distribution Agency
Al Galaa Street
Cairo
Tel: (20 2) 578-6083
Fax: (20 2) 578-6833

The Middle East Observer
41, Sherif Street
Cairo
Tel: (20 2) 393-9732
Fax: (20 2) 393-9732

FINLAND
Akateeminen Kirjakauppa
P.O. Box 128
FIN-00101 Helsinki
Tel: (358 0) 121 4418
Fax: (358 0) 121-4435
E-mail: akatilaus@stockmann.fi
URL: http://www.akateeminen.com

FRANCE
Editions Eska; DBJ
48, rue Gay Lussac
75005 Paris
Tel: (33-1) 55-42-73-08
Fax: (33-1) 43-29-91-67

GERMANY
UNO-Verlag
Poppelsdorfer Allee 55
53115 Bonn
Tel: (49 228) 949020
Fax: (49 228) 217492
URL: http://www.uno-verlag.de
E-mail: unoverlag@aol.com

GHANA
Epp Books Services
P.O. Box 44
TUC
Accra
Tel: 223 21 778843
Fax: 223 21 779099

GREECE
Papasotiriou S.A.
35, Stournara Str.
106 82 Athens
Tel: (30 1) 364-1826
Fax: (30 1) 364-8254

HAITI
Culture Diffusion
5, Rue Capois
C.P. 257
Port-au-Prince
Tel: (509) 23 9260
Fax: (509) 23 4858

HONG KONG, CHINA; MACAO
Asia 2000 Ltd.
Sales & Circulation Department
302 Seabird House
22-28 Wyndham Street, Central
Hong Kong, China
Tel: (852) 2530-1409
Fax: (852) 2526-1107
E-mail: sales@asia2000.com.hk
URL: http://www.asia2000.com.hk

HUNGARY
Euro Info Service
Margitszgeti Europa Haz
H-1138 Budapest
Tel: (36 1) 350 80 24, 350 80 25
Fax: (36 1) 350 90 32
E-mail: euroinfo@mail.matav.hu

INDIA
Allied Publishers Ltd.
751 Mount Road
Madras - 600 002
Tel: (91 44) 852-3938
Fax: (91 44) 852-0649

INDONESIA
Pt. Indira Limited
Jalan Borobudur 20
P.O. Box 181
Jakarta 10320
Tel: (62 21) 390-4290
Fax: (62 21) 390-4289

IRAN
Ketab Sara Co. Publishers
Khaled Eslamboli Ave., 6th Street
Delafrooz Alley No. 8
P.O. Box 15745-733
Tehran 15117
Tel: (98 21) 8717819; 8716104
Fax: (98 21) 8712479
E-mail: ketab-sara@neda.net.ir

Kowkab Publishers
P.O. Box 19575-511
Tehran
Tel: (98 21) 258-3723
Fax: (98 21) 258-3723

IRELAND
Government Supplies Agency
Oifig an tSolathair
4-5 Harcourt Road
Dublin 2
Tel: (353 1) 661-3111
Fax: (353 1) 475-2670

ISRAEL
Yozmot Literature Ltd.
P.O. Box 56055
3 Yohanan Hasandlar Street
Tel Aviv 61560
Tel: (972 3) 5285-397
Fax: (972 3) 5285-397

R.O.Y. International
PO Box 13056
Tel Aviv 61130
Tel: (972 3) 649 9469
Fax: (972 3) 648 6039
E-mail: royil@netvision.net.il
URL: http://www.royint.co.il

Palestinian Authority/Middle East
Index Information Services
P.O.B. 19502 Jerusalem
Tel: (972 2) 6271219
Fax: (972 2) 6271634

ITALY, LIBERIA
Licosa Commissionaria Sansoni SPA
Via Duca Di Calabria, 1/1
Casella Postale 552
50125 Firenze
Tel: (39 55) 645-415
Fax: (39 55) 641-257
E-mail: licosa@ftbcc.it
URL: http://www.ftbcc.it/licosa

JAMAICA
Ian Randle Publishers Ltd.
206 Old Hope Road, Kingston 6
Tel: 876-927-2085
Fax: 876-977-0243
E-mail: irpl@colis.com

JAPAN
Eastern Book Service
3-13 Hongo 3-chome, Bunkyo-ku
Tokyo 113
Tel: (81 3) 3818-0861
Fax: (81 3) 3818-0864
E-mail: orders@svt-ebs.co.jp
URL:
http://www.bekkoame.or.jp/~svt-ebs

KENYA
Africa Book Service (E.A.) Ltd.
Quaran House, Mfangano Street
P.O. Box 45245
Nairobi
Tel: (254 2) 223 641
Fax: (254 2) 330 272

Legacy Books
Loita House
Mezzanine 1
P.O. Box 68077
Nairobi
Tel: (254) 2-330853, 221426
Fax: (254) 2-330854, 561654
E-mail: Legacy@form-net.com

KOREA, REPUBLIC OF
Dayang Books Trading Co.
International Division
783-20, Pangba Bon-Dong,
Socho-ku
Seoul
Tel: (82 2) 536-9555
Fax: (82 2) 536-0025
E-mail: seamap@chollian.net

Eulyoo Publishing Co., Ltd.
46-1, Susong-Dong
Jongro-Gu
Seoul
Tel: (82 2) 734-3515
Fax: (82 2) 732-9154

LEBANON
Librairie du Liban
P.O. Box 11-9232
Beirut
Tel: (961 9) 217 944
Fax: (961 9) 217 434
E-mail: hsayegh@librairie-du-liban.com.lb
URL: http://www.librairie-du-liban.com.lb

MALAYSIA
University of Malaya Cooperative
Bookshop, Limited
P.O. Box 1127
Jalan Pantai Baru
59700 Kuala Lumpur
Tel: (60 3) 756-5000
Fax: (60 3) 755-4424
E-mail: umkoop@tm.net.my

MEXICO
INFOTEC
Av. San Fernando No. 37
Col. Toriello Guerra
14050 Mexico, D.F.
Tel: (52 5) 624-2800
Fax: (52 5) 624-2822
E-mail: infotec@rtn.net.mx
URL: http://rtn.net.mx

Mundi-Prensa Mexico S.A. de C.V.
c/Rio Panuco, 141-Colonia
Cuauhtemoc
06500 Mexico, D.F.
Tel: (52 5) 533-5658
Fax: (52 5) 514-6799

NEPAL
Everest Media International Services
(P.) Ltd.
GPO Box 5443
Kathmandu
Tel: (977 1) 416 026
Fax: (977 1) 224 431

NETHERLANDS
De Lindeboom/Internationale
Publicaties b.v.-
P.O. Box 202, 7480 AE Haaksbergen
Tel: (31 53) 574-0004
Fax: (31 53) 572-9296
E-mail: lindeboo@worldonline.nl
URL: http://www.worldonline.nl/~lin-deboo

NEW ZEALAND
EBSCO NZ Ltd.
Private Mail Bag 99914
New Market
Auckland
Tel: (64 9) 524-8119
Fax: (64 9) 524-8067

Oasis Official
P.O. Box 3627
Wellington
Tel: (64 4) 499 1551
Fax: (64 4) 499 1972
E-mail: oasis@actrix.gen.nz
URL: http://www.oasisbooks.co.nz/

NIGERIA
University Press Limited
Three Crowns Building Jericho
Private Mail Bag 5095
Ibadan
Tel: (234 22) 41-1356
Fax: (234 22) 41-2056

PAKISTAN
Mirza Book Agency
65, Shahrah-e-Quaid-e-Azam
Lahore 54000
Tel: (92 42) 735 3601
Fax: (92 42) 576 3714

Oxford University Press
5 Bangalore Town
Sharae Faisal
PO Box 13033
Karachi-75350
Tel: (92 21) 446307
Fax: (92 21) 4547640
E-mail: ouppak@TheOffice.net

Pak Book Corporation
Aziz Chambers 21, Queen's Road
Lahore
Tel: (92 42) 636 3222; 636 0885
Fax: (92 42) 636 2328
E-mail: pbc@brain.net.pk

PERU
Editorial Desarrollo SA
Apartado 3824, Ica 242 OF. 106
Lima 1
Tel: (51 14) 285380
Fax: (51 14) 286628

PHILIPPINES
International Booksource Center Inc.
1127-A Antipolo St, Barangay,
Venezuela
Makati City
Tel: (63 2) 896 6501; 6505; 6507
Fax: (63 2) 896 1741

POLAND
International Publishing Service
Ul. Piekna 31/37
00-677 Warzawa
Tel: (48 2) 628-6089
Fax: (48 2) 621-7255
E-mail: books%ips@ikp.atm.com.pl
URL:
http://www.ipscg.waw.pl/ips/export

PORTUGAL
Livraria Portugal
Apartado 2681, Rua Do Carm
o 70-74
1200 Lisbon
Tel: (1) 347-4982
Fax: (1) 347-0264

ROMANIA
Compani De Librarii Bucuresti S.A.
Str. Lipscani no. 26, sector 3
Bucharest
Tel: (40 1) 313 9645
Fax: (40 1) 312 4000

RUSSIAN FEDERATION
Isdatelstvo <Ves Mir>
9a, Kolpachniy Pereulok
Moscow 101831
Tel: (7 095) 917 87 49
Fax: (7 095) 917 92 59
ozimarin@glasnet.ru

**SINGAPORE; TAIWAN, CHINA
MYANMAR; BRUNEI**
Hemisphere Publication Services
41 Kallang Pudding Road #04-03
Golden Wheel Building
Singapore 349316
Tel: (65) 741-5166
Fax: (65) 742-9356
E-mail: ashgate@asianconnect.com

SLOVENIA
Gospodarski vestnik Publishing
Group
Dunajska cesta 5
1000 Ljubljana
Tel: (386 61) 133 83 47; 132 12 30
Fax: (386 61) 133 80 30
E-mail: repansekj@gvestnik.si

SOUTH AFRICA, BOTSWANA
For single titles:
Oxford University Press Southern
Africa
Vasco Boulevard, Goodwood
P.O. Box 12119, N1 City 7463
Cape Town
Tel: (27 21) 595 4400
Fax: (27 21) 595 4430
E-mail: oxford@oup.co.za

For subscription orders:
International Subscription Service
P.O. Box 41095
Craighall
Johannesburg 2024
Tel: (27 11) 880-1448
Fax: (27 11) 880-6248
E-mail: iss@is.co.za

SPAIN
Mundi-Prensa Libros, S.A.
Castello 37
28001 Madrid
Tel: (34 91) 4 363700
Fax: (34 91) 5 753998
E-mail: libreria@mundiprensa.es
URL: http://www.mundiprensa.com/

Mundi-Prensa Barcelona
Consell de Cent, 391
08009 Barcelona
Tel: (34 3) 488-3492
Fax: (34 3) 487-7659
E-mail: barcelona@mundiprensa.es

SRI LANKA, THE MALDIVES
Lake House Bookshop
100, Sir Chittampalam Gardiner
Mawatha
Colombo 2
Tel: (94 1) 32105
Fax: (94 1) 432104
E-mail: LHL@sri.lanka.net

SWEDEN
Wennergren-Williams AB
P. O. Box 1305
S-171 25 Solna
Tel: (46 8) 705-97-50
Fax: (46 8) 27-00-71
E-mail: mail@wwi.se

SWITZERLAND
Librairie Payot Service Institutionnel
C(tm)tes-de-Montbenon 30
1002 Lausanne
Tel: (41 21) 341-3229
Fax: (41 21) 341-3235

ADECO Van Diermen
EditionsTechniques
Ch. de Lacuez 41
CH1807 Blonay
Tel: (41 21) 943 2673
Fax: (41 21) 943 3605

THAILAND
Central Books Distribution
306 Silom Road
Bangkok 10500
Tel: (66 2) 2336930-9
Fax: (66 2) 237-8321

**TRINIDAD & TOBAGO
AND THE CARRIBBEAN**
Systematics Studies Ltd.
St. Augustine Shopping Center
Eastern Main Road, St. Augustine
Trinidad & Tobago, West Indies
Tel: (868) 645-8466
Fax: (868) 645-8467
E-mail: tobe@trinidad.net

UGANDA
Gustro Ltd.
PO Box 9997, Madhvani Building
Plot 16/4 Jinja Rd.
Kampala
Tel: (256 41) 251 467
Fax: (256 41) 251 468
E-mail: gus@swiftuganda.com

UNITED KINGDOM
Microinfo Ltd.
P.O. Box 3, Omega Park, Alton,
Hampshire GU34 2PG
England
Tel: (44 1420) 86848
Fax: (44 1420) 89889
E-mail: wbank@microinfo.co.uk
URL: http://www.microinfo.co.uk

The Stationery Office
51 Nine Elms Lane
London SW8 5DR
Tel: (44 171) 873-8400
Fax: (44 171) 873-8242
URL: http://www.the-stationery-office.co.uk/

VENEZUELA
Tecni-Ciencia Libros, S.A.
Centro Cuidad Comercial Tamanco
Nivel C2, Caracas
Tel: (58 2) 959 5547; 5035; 0016
Fax: (58 2) 959 5636

ZAMBIA
University Bookshop, University of
Zambia
Great East Road Campus
P.O. Box 32379
Lusaka
Tel: (260 1) 252 576
Fax: (260 1) 253 952

ZIMBABWE
Academic and Baobab Books (Pvt.)
Ltd.
4 Conald Road, Graniteside
P.O. Box 567
Harare
Tel: 263 4 755035
Fax: 263 4 781913

DATE DUE

			Printed in USA

HIGHSMITH #45230

Recent World Bank Technical Papers (*continued*)

No. 443 Luc Lecuit, John Elder, Christian Hurtado, François Rantrua, Kamal Siblini, and Maurizia Tovo, *DeMIStifying MIS: Guidelines for Management Information Systems in Social Funds*

No. 444 Robert F. Townsend, *Agricultural Incentives in Sub-Saharan Africa: Policy Challenges*

No. 445 Ian Hill, *Forest Management in Nepal: Economics of Ecology*

No. 446 Gordon Hughes and Magda Lovei, *Economic Reform and Environmental Performance in Transition Economies*

No. 447 R. Maria Saleth and Ariel Dinar, *Evaluating Water Institutions and Water Sector Performance*

No. 449 Keith Oblitas and J. Raymond Peter in association with Gautam Pingle, Halla M. Qaddumi, and Jayantha Perera, *Transferring Irrigation Management to Farmers in Andhra Pradesh, India*

No. 450 Andrés Rigo Sureda and Waleed Haider Malik, eds., *Judicial Challenges in the New Millennium: Proceedings of the Second Summit of the Ibero-American Supreme Courts*

No. 451 World Bank, *Privatization of the Power and Natural Gas Industries in Hungary and Kazakhstan*

No. 452 Lev Freinkman, Daniel Treisman, and Stephen Titov, *Subnational Budgeting in Russia: Preempting a Potential Crisis*

No. 453 Bartlomiej Kaminski and Michelle Riboud, *Foreign Investment and Restructuring: The Evidence from Hungary*

No. 454 Gordon Hughes and Julia Bucknall, *Poland: Complying with EU Environmental Legislature*

No. 455 Dale F. Gray, *Assessment of Corporate Sector Value and Vulnerability: Links to Exchange Rate and Financial Crises*

No. 456 Salman M.A. Salman, ed., *Groundwater: Legal and Policy Perspectives: Proceedings of a World Bank Seminar*

No. 457 Mary Canning, Peter Moock, and Timothy Heleniak, *Reforming Education in the Regions of Russia*

No. 458 John Gray, *Kazakhstan: A Review of Farm Restructuring*

No. 459 Zvi Lerman and Csaba Csaki, *Ukraine: Review of Farm Restructuring Experiences*

No. 460 Gloria La Cava and Rafaella Y. Nanetti, *Albania: Filling the Vulnerability Gap*

No. 461 Ayse Kudat, Stan Peabody, and Caglar Keyder, eds., *Social Assessment and Agricultural Reform in Central Asia and Turkey*

No. 462 T. Rand, J. Haukohl, and U. Marxen, *Municipal Solid Waste Incineration: Requirements for a Successful Project*

No. 463 Stephen Foster, John Chilton, Marcus Moench, Franklin Cardy, and Manuel Schiffler, *Groundwater in Rural Development: Facing the Challenges of Supply and Resource Sustainability*

No. 465 Csaba Csaki and Zvi Lerman, eds., *Structural Change in the Farming Sectors in Central and Eastern Europe: Lessons for EU Accession—Second World Bank/ FAO Workshop, June 27–29, 1999*

No. 466 Barbara Nunberg, *Ready for Europe: Public Administration Reform and European Union Accession in Central and Eastern Europe*

No. 467 Quentin T. Wodon with contributions from Robert Ayres, Matias Barenstein, Norman Hicks, Kihoon Lee, William Maloney, Pia Peeters, Corinne Siaens, and Shlomo Yitzhaki, *Poverty and Policy in Latin America and the Caribbean*

No. 469 Laurian Unnevehr and Nancy Hirschhorn, *Food Safety Issues in the Developing World*

No. 470 Alberto Valdés, ed., *Agricultural Support Policies in Transition Economies*

No. 471 Brian Pinto, Vladimir Drebentsov, and Alexander Morozov, *Dismantling Russia's Nonpayments System: Creating Conditions for Growth*

No. 472 Jit B. S. Gill, *A Diagnostic Framework for Revenue Administration*

No. 473 Esen Ulgenerk and Leila Zlaoui, *From Transition to Accession: Developing Stable and Competitive Financial Markets in Bulgaria*

No. 474 Ioannis N. Kessides, ed., *Hungary: A Regulatory and Structural Review of Selected Infrastructure Sectors*

No. 475 Csaba Csaki, Zvi Lerman, and Sergey Sotnikov, *Farm Sector Restructuring in Belarus: Progress and Constraints*

No. 481 Csaba Csaki, John Nash, Achim Fock, and Holger Kray, *Food and Agriculture in Bulgaria: The Challenge of Preparing for EU Accession*

No. 484 Csaba Csaki and Laura Tuck, *Rural Development Strategy: Eastern Europe and Central Asia*

No. 488 Nina Bubnova, *Governance Impact on Private Investment*

No. 489 Tim Schwarz and David Satola, *Telecommunications Legislation in Transitional and Developing Economies*

THE WORLD BANK

1818 H Street, N.W.
Washington, D.C. 20433 U.S.A.

Telephone: 202-477-1234

Facsimile: 202-477-6391

Telex: MCI 64145 WORLDBANK
      MCI 248423 WORLDBANK

Internet: www.worldbank.org

E-mail: books@worldbank.org

14796

9 780821 347966

ISBN 0-8213-4796-